WORKING IN THE
MUSIC
INDUSTRY

If you want to know how . . .

How to get a Job in Television
Insider secrets you need to get and keep your dream job in TV

Getting into Films & Television
How to spot the opportunities and find the best way in

Passing Psychometric Tests
Know what to expect and get the job you want

howtobooks

For full details, please send for a free copy of the
latest catalogue to:
How To Books
Spring Hill House, Spring Hill Road
Begbroke, Oxford OX5 1RX
info@howtobooks.co.uk
www.howtobooks.co.uk

WORKING IN THE MUSIC INDUSTRY

HOW TO FIND AN EXCITING AND VARIED CAREER IN THE WORLD OF MUSIC

ANNA BRITTEN

With a foreword by ALAN McGEE

REVISED AND UPDATED · SECOND EDITION · 2ND

howtobooks

Published by How To Books Ltd
Spring Hill House, Spring Hill Road
Begbroke, Oxford OX5 1RX
Tel: (01865) 375794. Fax: (01865) 379162
email: info@howtobooks.co.uk
www.howtobooks.co.uk

First edition 2004
Second edition 2006

British Library Cataloguing in Publication Data
A catalogue record for this book is available from the British
Library

ISBN 13: 978-1-84528-154-0
ISBN 10: 1-84528-154-3

Cover design by Baseline Arts Ltd, Oxford
Produced for How To Books by Deer Park Productions,
Tavistock, Devon
Typeset by TW Typesetting, Plymouth, Devon
Printed and bound by Cromwell Press, Trowbridge, Wiltshire

Contents

Preface

You've probably picked up this book because you'd like a job in the music industry. Join the queue. Thousands of music-loving students and school leavers every year dream of a career surrounded by pop, rock, jazz, folk or classical music.

Who could blame you? The music industry is a place you'll find excitement, glamour, fun, creativity, passion and, at the risk of sounding corny, the occasional utterly transcendental moment of sheer bliss. But be warned, you'll also find exhaustion, frustration, swollen egos, depression, poor pay and buckets of stress. Only a profound and unwavering love of music will get you through all that intact, so don't even think about a career in this industry unless you have it.

You may know exactly what kind of job you want and how to get it – good for you. However, even those who think they know what a job in the 'music biz' entails, and feel they are up to the challenge, can't lay their hands on much practical information on how to break into what is a highly competitive field, and what to expect when they're there. A lot of the advice out there fires you up but leaves you asking: but how, exactly, do I do it? That's where this book comes in.

Maybe you doubt your abilities but simply know you can't imagine working in any other industry. This book aims to show you that fun and rewarding jobs in the world of music are within the grasp of almost anyone with a true passion for music and a hard-working attitude. Opportunities arise constantly, everywhere from the cut-and-thrust of a central London record company to the sweat-and-sawdust of a provincial live music venue.

This is not a book about making it as a musician, but explores the jobs and people in the *background* of every pop star, rock band or world-famous conductor. Each possible career area is covered and is sprinkled liberally with case studies of people ascending the career ladder in their chosen field. Many of these are young people whose example you can aspire to – not just lofty big figures who started their careers when offices were full of typewriters.

Most fields within the music industry are covered, but by no means all. I have not covered jobs in radio or TV as these industries need a whole book of their own (see How To Books' list of publications on page ii) and are not purely about music. The music industry sprawls huge distances in various directions across so many fields that to encompass it all would be impossible in one book, but the main job areas are covered.

Working in the Music Industry aims to be brutally honest, realistic, practical and full of insider secrets. Whatever I haven't learned from my own experience of working within various fields of the music industry – from a major record company to music magazines – I have gleaned straight from the horse's mouth. And as that horse's mouth tends to spout a fair amount of industry jargon, there's even a handy glossary at the end.

Time and again the people interviewed have repeated the same message: if you believe passionately in something, stick with it.

This book is for you whether you intend to become chairman of Sony Music or the roadie of choice for your favourite local band. Whether you want to earn £100k, or are happy with £10k. It doesn't matter whether you are destined to be a great big cheese or just a Dairylea triangle – if you worship music and can't think of anything better than being immersed in it all day, somewhere there's a place for you.

Anna Britten

Acknowledgements

Many thanks to:

The Agency Group
Bob Angus
Nathan Beazer
Elena Bello
Jakub Blackman
Matthew Cosgrove
Peter and Freddie Coulson
Dave Higgitt, *Venue* magazine
Paul Lloyd
Alan McGee
Alison Millar
Lisa Moskaluk
Sharon O'Connell
Tim Orchard
Angela Penhaligon
Nikki Read
Chris Salmon
James Smith
Dimitri Tikovoi
Antony Topping
Mark Vernon
Andy Woolliscroft

Foreword
by Alan McGee

The music business is one of the few industries left, for the working classes in Britain, where education doesn't dictate success or failure. A musical instinct is what matters. Whether you think The Hives are good, or Blue a manufactured piece of garbage, at the end of the day it's one of the few industries left where instinct plays the largest part in most people's success.

So many times in the last 20 years (God, I sound like an old-age pensioner), whenever I have been written off or rubbished by the critics, the only thing that has saved me from the musical abyss – whether working with The Jesus And Mary Chain in 1984 or The Hives in 2002 – is my passion for and love of music.

The best advice I could give any young person starting off in the music industry is: go and listen to as much music as you can, and gather as much information as you can about it. While my colleagues at school in Glasgow in 1975 were readying themselves for O-levels, I was holed up in my bedroom listening to 'The Rise And Fall Of Ziggy Stardust And The Spiders From Mars'. David Bowie and Ziggy, to this day, have never failed me.

Always follow your musical instincts – they are probably not wrong. In the past, any time I have based a deal about music on money or political status within a record company it has always backfired on me. Yet whenever I've signed a band because I just happened to love them it's had a happy ending, artistically or financially: My Bloody Valentine's 'Loveless' was the greatest rock record made in the 90s, and Oasis's 'What's the Story, Morning Glory?' was the biggest selling album in Great Britain in the 90s, selling 4.5 million copies. Those two successes, both within the same label, were each a one-off scenario as far as I or anyone else was concerned.

My advice is pretty simple: never give in. The next person who walks through your door could be the superstar for the next generation. And remember: always be nice to the receptionist. They could end up running Radio One in four years' time.

Alan McGee

An Overview of the Music Industry

In this chapter:

- ◆ Is the music industry right for you?

- ◆ Deciding which field to go for

- ◆ The structure of the music industry

IS THE MUSIC INDUSTRY RIGHT FOR YOU?
Do you love music?

I mean, do you *really* love music? It's fine to listen mainly to your favourite bands or genres, but it's really not enough to be a one-album-a-year type of person. You need to be the sort of person who buys albums on a regular basis, knows what's going on in the charts, who's hot, who's not. Music has to be an essential part of your life. If you're unsure whether this is the case for you, ask yourself the following:

- ◆ Has music ever brought tears to your eyes?

- ◆ Do you ever sit people down on the edge of your bed and force them to listen to a particular song?

- ◆ Have you ever been first in the queue to buy a new

album or concert ticket the very minute it went on sale?

If you've said yes to two out of three, read on.

Do you know enough about music?

You may have been the school authority on underground speed garage, or be the best young harpist in the North-West. That's great – play to your skills, because they'll mark you out as an individual. But don't be blinkered: you also need to know a bit of musical history and be familiar with other genres to be taken seriously; you need to spread your options. You don't have to *like* David Bowie, Mozart, The Rolling Stones, The Beatles, Johnny Cash, Public Enemy or The Cheeky Girls but you really have to know who they are. This is where your mum, dad and grandparents (oh yes) can come in handy. If they aren't busy trying to talk you out of a career in the music industry and into becoming a doctor instead, that is.

What kind of salary do you expect?

Think of the lowest salary you can imagine surviving on and halve it. That's probably what you'll be earning in the beginning. It's a myth that everyone in the music biz drives a Merc, holidays in their villa near Nice and dines at The Ivy every night. Sure, some do. But it took them many years to get to that point. Ask any big cheese and chances are you'll find someone who remembers all too clearly starting out as a poorly-paid secretary, reception-ist or warehouse operative.

Many jobs in the music industry will require that you have acquired skills and experience through work experience – which is unpaid. Even having survived that financial challenge, most entry-level jobs start at between £10k and £16k, maybe less. Bear in mind that a low salary is not just about struggling to pay the rent and living on cheap white bread. It's about holding your head up when all your friends from school or college are doing very nicely thank you in banks, schools or law firms and making twice the money you are, buying cars and clothes while you're turning up late to get-togethers in the pub because you can't afford to buy more than one round. Can you hack it? Good for you!

Can you work hard enough?
So it's not quite as tiring as being a junior doctor, but the music industry's insistence upon unpaid overtime, evening and weekend work commitments, microscopically short lunch breaks, crazy deadlines and lots of stress will take their toll on anyone without the requisite energy or ingrained work ethic. It also requires you to start at the bottom of the heap. Anyone leaving university feeling snootily disinclined to fix photocopier jams, do the coffee run or stuff envelopes for hours will be given very, very, very short shrift in this business.

Don't be fooled into thinking that just because the average working day in the music industry starts at 10am (but most people don't actually turn up until half past . . .) it's an easy ride. The late mornings are usually a result of late nights spent either in the office or on-duty at gigs (never really relaxing if you're there in an official capacity). Factor in also any supplementary activities you might be doing on the side to stay afloat, or just to keep your finger on the pulse. People in music industry jobs often end up writing for websites, promoting gigs, playing in bands or doing weekend jobs in their spare time.

Can you handle the competition?

Few experiences are more daunting than sitting in a swanky record company reception with a load of other suited-and-booted young hopefuls all chasing the same super-cool job. This feeling never really goes away completely, even when you've worked somewhere for years and know all the security staff by their first names. There will always be someone in the company – maybe more than one person – after your job. Might be a girl on the floor below, might be the chap sitting next to you who you play footie with every Tuesday night. Outside the company there's even more competition. Every day, human resources departments in music industry organisations get on-spec applications of ever increasing quality. You put one foot wrong, slack off, make mistakes – and you could be out on your ear. Employers in the music industry can afford to be hard on their staff.

Are you a 'people person'?

It's generally fair to say that the people who get along best in the music industry are those who team hard work and enthusiasm with being, for want of a better word, nice. Friendly, chatty, helpful, reliable and good fun people – who also put the work in – are always welcome. It's the empty-headed egotists, directionless mavericks and plain nasty cut-throats who tend to be in and out of the revolving doors in a flash.

WHICH FIELD?

Different fields call for different skills, personality types and experience. These individual requirements will be explained in more detail in later chapters.

Pop, rock or classical?

If you're in a quandary about where to target your music biz ambitions, have a think primarily about whether you would like to work in **classical** or **pop/rock**. At the risk of generalising hugely and possibly offending a lot of people in both fields (deep breath) . . . the classical industry tends to be more sedate, intellectual and musically purist, with smaller sales and therefore a bit less stress. Pop/rock is more out-and-out hip, thrusting, commercial and dog-eat-dog. (Other genres like **jazz**, **world** and **folk music** are usually incorporated under either the banner 'pop' or 'classical' when it comes to the structure of a record company and fall somewhere between the two.)

Back-stage or front-of-house?

Once you've chosen your musical field, think about whether you're a back-room sort of person or a showman. If you are the former and like to keep your head down and get stuck into your work with as little interference from or contact with the outside world as possible, you might flourish in manufacturing, rights administration, human resources, sound engineering, roadying, design and production, or product management.

However, if you're a bit of a performer yourself, consider a career in sales, marketing, PR, A & R, artist management or concert promoting.

If you still can't decide, just go through the chapters in this book one by one and see what leaps out.

'Indie' spirit or corporate beast?

Are you a hard-nosed business type or an artistic free-spirit? Actually, that's a trick question: you need to be a mixture of the two, ideally. But it's worth thinking about whether you'll thrive in the high-end, money-driven environment of a commercial record label whose music you might never personally be caught listening to in a million years, or whether you'd be happier in a small label where the financial expectations – and therefore capitalist dogma, comrades! – are fewer and you adore the product.

THE STRUCTURE OF THE MUSIC INDUSTRY

'The music industry' is an umbrella term that covers a myriad of different operations. The one thing they have in common is that they all orbit around and support the band or artist, who in turn fuels them. Aside from the artists, jobs fall into three loose categories: **recording**, **publishing** and **live music**.

Every job within the industry is inextricably linked to several others in a symbiotic relationship that involves a lot of schmoozing, 'plus ones' and tactical voicemail deployment.

The diagram below illustrates how relationships between companies and individuals in the music business work. You will find each job mentioned below featured somewhere in this book.

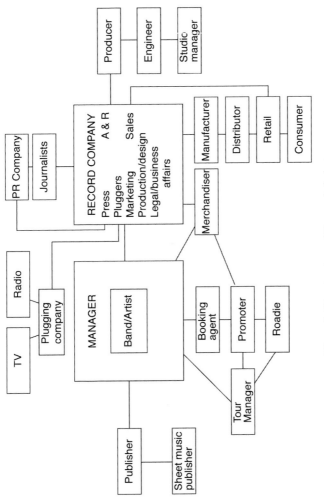

Figure 1. The structure of the music industry.

(2)

Getting a Job

In this chapter:

♦ How to improve your chances

♦ Where to find out about vacancies

♦ Making contacts in the industry

♦ Preparing for an interview

There's no easy, normal or traditional way to get a job in the music industry. You may read all the suggestions in this book and then end up getting a job because you spilt a drink on a record producer at your neighbour's barbecue.

Whether it's a major record label or a small recording studio, many of the same principles for getting a foot in the door apply. What follows in this chapter is a series of tips on getting jobs that apply to almost all sectors of the industry – work experience, for example, is a good idea whatever job you're eventually after. Many of the same 'ways in' apply, so rather than repeat the same things in every separate chapter I've listed them all here in one handy reference guide. But for more specialist tips on impressing potential employers in a particular field you should refer to the relevant individual chapters *as well as* using the pointers in this chapter.

Unfortunately, entry-level jobs in the music business are few and far between, and many vacancies are only publicised by word of mouth. Many people are 'poached' from elsewhere in the music industry. So what can you do?

To maximise your chances of success, try a multi-pronged attack consisting of all the following.

(For all contact details Useful Addresses on page 142.)

BEFORE YOU START . . .

You won't get far without a copy of the industry bible, the *Music Week Directory* (see Useful Addresses and Further Reading), an exhaustive list of every music industry contact you'll ever need. If your local library or careers service hasn't got a copy you will have little choice but to invest in one. At £65 it isn't cheap, but it is worth it.

The Useful Addresses section has contact info for most of the main players and companies mentioned in this book.

You'll also find it very handy to have access to the weekly trade magazine *Music Week* (yes, publisher of the above), available from larger newsagents or libraries or by subscription.

AT COLLEGE/UNIVERSITY/SCHOOL

Become a member of the entertainments committee, ball committee, or even better the Social Secretary or its equivalent. I won't pretend this is always easy – in many universities this alone can be as competitive as getting a job! So if the cliques have it all sewn up round your way, do something like:

- Form your own band or promote other people's

- Set up your own society devoted to your own favourite genre of music

- Go to gigs

- Buy, download or borrow plenty of music

- Read the music press

- Start a fanzine/webzine

- DJ

- Start up and promote your own club night.

COURSES

It must be mentioned here that the majority of employers within the music industry are not overly impressed by academic qualifications unless they are backed up with relevant experience and the right sort of personality. If you merely do a course and expect that to open doors, you will be sorely disappointed. That said, certain courses related to the music industry are pretty essential for some jobs – sound engineering and other technical skills for example. And even the more theoretical subjects will give you great support when in the workplace.

There are far too many courses on or related to the music industry to list here – more than 500 different courses at over 150 colleges and universities at the last count. These range from GCSEs right up to MAs and can be part-time, full-time, face-to-face or correspondence courses.

◆ The British Phonographic Industry (BPI) has a huge database of these courses. See **www.bpi-med.co.uk** or badger your careers advice centre to purchase the *BPI Music Education Directory*.

◆ Phone or log on to Learn Direct.

◆ Your local education authority will have details of relevant courses in your area.

WORK EXPERIENCE AND STUDENT PLACEMENTS

Contact companies you are interested in and offer to do **unpaid work experience**, showing a willingness to undertake anything they throw at you. A lot of companies are grateful for the help – many permanently have a work experience person helping out in the office, each staying for a few weeks at a time. If you're fortunate enough to get work experience somewhere, slog your heart out, make friends and make the most of it. Afterwards, stay in touch, stay interested in them, keep emphasising how keen you are, and if a job comes along you'll stand a chance of being in the right place at the right time.

Short-term and long-term **student placements** are available at many record companies. They are nearly always unpaid but expenses such as travel costs and food are often refunded. Send a CV, covering letter and details of availability to the human resources department, marking it 'Work Experience' to ensure it gets to the right person in the quickest possible time.

The *Music Week* 'Jobs and Courses' section regularly features ads for internships and work experience slots.

GRADUATE RECRUITMENT

Look out for recruitment fairs at your college or university, check the *Guardian* graduate and creative/media jobs sections and keep an eye on the major companies' websites.

You're not going to walk out of a fair with a job: it's just for information about vacancies and graduate recruitment schemes really, but if you make the most of it you'll walk out with more than just a company brochure. Arrive in good time – not too early, definitely not last through the door just as everyone's looking forward to getting home, and not over lunchtime if you can help it.

Take a CV and a big smile and talk to as many people as you can. The first thing you'll notice is the big scrum around the A & R and promotions departments' stalls as some hapless employee tries to talk to 25 clamouring wannabes all at the same time. This is not only unnerving it's also an inefficient use of your time. So don't be a sheep, be clever – go talk to someone else. Pick the brains of someone in a less frantic corner like classics or business affairs, find out as much as you can about the company, who's who, and make friends.

When it comes to graduate recruitment, never forget that a good degree is not enough. You *must* back this up with experience, just as a non-graduate would have to.

TEMPING

If you can get out of bed and be ready for the office at short notice of a morning, temping is a brilliant way to start. So if you have all the basic necessary skills (typing, knowledge of main software packages, good interpersonal skills and command of English, etc.) contact one of the temping agencies that supply London record companies, such as Handle PR (see Useful Addresses). They supply temps to most majors and indies when members of staff are ill or on holiday, and if you send them a CV and covering letter, and have some useful experience, you could end up being sent by them to all sorts of exciting music industry hotspots. See their website **www.handle.co.uk**.

Two other favoured music biz temping agencies are The Music Market and Career Moves (see Useful Addresses).

WHERE TO FIND OUT ABOUT VACANCIES

- Company websites
- *Music Week*
- The Monday edition of the *Guardian*'s creative and media jobs section
- Dig out addresses of companies from the *Music Week Directory* (see Useful Addresses and Further Reading) and send on-spec CVs and letters
- Specialist websites such as **www.uk.music-jobs.com**.

JUNIOR PRESS OFFICER

required for small funky music PR company. Enthusiasm, self-motivation, and a great communicator essential, as is knowledge of music. Previous experience in PR or journalism is beneficial. Salary based on experience.

Email CV and covering letter to:
lisa@idpublicity.com

metropolis group

RECEPTIONIST

Metropolis Group are looking for a self-motivated and organised person to join our large Media Facility in West London. The ideal candidate will have minimum 6 months' switchboard experience and a confident, bubbly yet polite personality.

Hours: Mon >Fri 09:00-18:30.

Please send CVs to **jobs@metropolis-group.co.uk**

Figure 2. Entry-level job ads. Please note these ads are for illustration only and are not current vacancies.

SUGGESTED FILL-IN JOBS

Assuming you don't have a trust fund, wealthy spouse or hyper-indulgent parents, you will need something to tide you over whilst you wangle your wily way into a proper music industry job. If circumstances allow, the following will all look somewhat more impressive on your CV than launderette attendant:

- Working in a record store (the number one option – see also Chapter 10)

- Working in a musical instrument or sheet music shop

- Any sort of events/promotion work

- Box office or ticket agency staff

- Bar staff at music venue

- Customer services

- Working in a CD distributor's warehouse (see Chapter 3)

- Sales rep.

NETWORK, NETWORK, NETWORK . . .

Ah, the most elusive part of the whole job-seeking process. You need **contacts**. This is all very well if you move in the sort of hip, happenin' circles where everyone knows someone who knows a pop star. But if you're straight out of rural Northumberland and all your friends are primary school teachers, where on earth do you start? Don't be scared – networking or 'making contacts' is just a daft, modern way of saying 'making friends' or 'striking up acquaintances'. So, make friends. It starts with a hello, offering someone a light or asking for the time. It moves on to talking about music, generally chewing the fat and hopefully ends up with your face lodged in the memory and your number in the Nokia. Don't stalk, don't hassle, don't butt in like a big, fat pain in the rear; just try to fit in, be your normal likeable music-loving self and **make friends**.

So, here's where to find music industry people:

- **Industry get-togethers**: Midem (more on page 35) in Cannes, France, or In the City, Manchester

- **Columbia Hotel**, London. Where nearly all the visiting bands stay. Therefore full of industry types and journos too

- **Awards ceremonies** (you'll have to try to win tickets as entry will be by invite only)

- Any decent **pub** close to your chosen ideal workplace

- **The bars of important gig venues**, especially the upstairs bar of the Shepherds Bush Empire, where all the journos, PRs, and record execs hang out before, during and after the show.

PREPARING FOR AN INTERVIEW

A time will surely come when all of the above efforts pay off and you start submitting applications for jobs for which you feel relatively confident of at least getting an interview. Of course you already satisfy the criteria in Chapter 1. So at this stage you should now also:

- **Listen to music** – old, new, stuff you like, stuff other people like but you don't know why, stuff you hate . . . You don't have to spend a fortune. Many artists' websites have free tracks you can download. Libraries lend CDs and stores have listening posts on which you can hear new releases for free. If they tell you to get a move on, tell them your leg's gone into a seizure.

◆ **Read interviews and articles** in *Music Week* about industry figures and note down names. If a name appears more than once you know this is an important person.

◆ **Research** *thoroughly* the company and what they do. Employers hate it when candidates are too vague about their aims and instead just say they want to work 'somewhere in the music industry'. You've got to want to work for *them* specifically.

Dressing for an interview

As a cursory glance around the offices of most music-based companies will prove, every day is dress-down Friday in the music business. As a general rule, you can wear whatever you like to work – jeans and trainers even. But for an interview, be it for a fledgling start-up or a global corporation, smart-casual is recommended. Dress as you would if you were meeting friends for lunch. While there's no need to be a fashion-slave, don't look like you're completely clueless about current fashions either. So if you do opt for a suit, avoid looking like a petrified librarian by selecting a trendy shirt or cool record bag to take the edge off it.

NB: There are exceptions! International headquarters of major record companies, legal and accountancy departments, plus any jobs in which you are the 'public face' of the company (e.g. sales jobs) are often a little smarter – so play safe. Still unsure? Loiter inconspicuously at the company's front door around 10 am one day and note what employees are wearing.

Attitude

Friendly, streetwise confidence is key. During your interview, bear in mind the traditional rules of interview etiquette, but also be aware that this is the entertainment industry and thus not constrained by the rules and customs of, say, a merchant bank or legal firm. So roll your shoulders back, loosen up and walk into the room determined to give the impression you are happy and self-confident, resilient, flexible, loyal and hard-working. Humour is welcome, but don't overdo it. Be intelligent, but not arrogant or nerdy. In fact, behave as well as you would on a first date with someone extremely gorgeous, rich and clever. Just be your own lovable self.

Dos and don'ts

- Don't say, 'I just want to get into the music industry somehow'.

- Don't name-drop.

- Don't fawn or gush.

- Don't swear, yawn, smoke or chew gum.

- Do express your interest in and talent for marketing/talent-spotting/number-crunching/journalist-courting/plane ticket-booking [delete as applicable].

- Do know the name of the company chief, and the names of those interviewing you.

- Do smile.

- Do have an iPod, or a personal stereo and a few good CDs poking out of the top of your bag.

Some favourite music industry interview questions

- What was the last CD you bought?

- What was the last gig you went to?

- What are your favourite top ten albums and why? (This isn't necessarily to judge your musical taste, it's to measure your passion for music and ability to convince others.)

Psychometric tests

Many larger companies have now introduced psychometric, numeracy and literacy tests as part of their recruitment procedure. Just how much value these have in determining a person's suitability for a job is doubtful, and many employers only go through with them to appease their Human Resources Director. The face-to-face interview remains the most important element of the procedure. However, you may like to brush up your maths and English skills with one of the many books on the market that contain sample tests; and as for the psychometric test, just be honest (but not too honest).

Record Companies

In this chapter:

♦ What do record companies do?

♦ Different types of record companies

♦ Things you need to know

♦ Different departments within a record company

♦ Getting in the door

♦ Manufacturers

♦ Distributors

WHAT DO RECORD COMPANIES DO?

Record companies are the organisations that turn musical ideas from tunes inside a musician's head into the shiny discs playing on your stereo, and the files on your iPod. They make and distribute records: singles and albums on CD (sometimes vinyl but hardly ever cassette nowadays). Releases are also available as a paid-for digital download from the internet. Money is also made from merchandise, ringtones for mobile phones and selling music for use in advertising, films, TV and computer games and other bits and bobs.

Records are one of the strands through which musicians make money, and are – with the possible exception of classical records – arguably the most lucrative. Bands and artists are headhunted by, and sign contracts with, record companies: perhaps for just one album, perhaps for several if they've got potential or a good track record. The record company organises **recording** or **remixing** of their music (a small proportion of 'demos' will be put out, if they are of high enough quality) and turns this into records. They produce any amount from a limited run of 50, to an initial pressing of 50,000 or more if it's the new Robbie Williams album, and send these to a **distributor** – sometimes another wing of the record company, sometimes a separate company which may distribute records from several different companies. The distributor then sells them to shops. The record company crosses its fingers and hopes it has a hit on its hands. A myriad of different departments are responsible for seeing this process through. They are addressed later in this chapter.

The legal download market
Record companies also sell music through online distributors such as OD2 (who supply 'e-retailers' such as MSN, Wanadoo, MTV and Tiscali) and MusicNet (which supplies AOL and HMV's online operation) plus iTunes and Napster, which sell directly to individuals. See also page 24.

Record companies do not deal solely with new recordings. Much work is done on 'exploiting **back catalogue**', which means dreaming up new ways to sell old music. This might mean repackaging it with a new sleeve and

advertising campaign; creating a compilation of an artist's greatest hits, or of various artists' songs, perhaps
under a 'theme' such as love songs for Valentine's Day,
or that old chestnut, 'Christmas Hits'.

And don't forget classical music – someone has to make
and sell all those Beethoven's Fifths, you know.

WHAT IS THE BPI?

Record companies are represented by the trade organisation the British Phonographic Industry (BPI). If you
recognise the name that's probably because it funds the
BRIT Awards, lobbies Parliament and supplies information to the media on the British record industry. Their
website is an invaluable resource for anyone seeking a job
in the music biz, so do check it out (see Useful Addresses).

DIFFERENT TYPES OF RECORD COMPANIES

At time of going to print there are four major record
companies. These are known, unimaginatively, as 'the
majors', and a little knowledge about them can be very
impressive when it comes to an interview situation. At
present the biggies are:

- Sony BMG (which owns Arista, Columbia, Epic, Jive,
  RCA and others)

- EMI (which owns Capitol, EMI:Chrysalis, Parlo-
  phone, Hut, Innocent, Virgin, Source, EMI Classics
  and others)

- Universal (which owns Mercury, Island, Polydor,
  Decca, Deutsche Grammophon and others)

◆ Warner (which owns Atlantic, Elektra, Nonesuch, Blanco Y Negro, Warner Classics, East West, London and others).

Majors often own several small labels, many of which discover and record talent themselves. Fred Durst's Interscope label, for example, looks on the surface as if it is all his, but it is bankrolled and distributed by Universal.

Majors also tend to own their own distribution companies (i.e. the people who take orders, pack boxes, and send the CDs off to your local record shop), distributing their own wares plus other companies' (which pay them for this service).

Beneath these come those record companies that go it alone and are not part of a major label. These are privately owned and financed by owners/investors, and are called **independents** or **indie** labels. Important ones include the likes of Domino (Franz Ferdinand, Arctic Monkeys and others), XL (The White Stripes, Dizzee Rascal and others), B-Unique (Kaiser Chiefs, The Ordinary Boys and others), Ministry Of Sound, Rough Trade ... and in the classical corner the mammoth Naxos, widely regarded as the most successful classical music label in the world.

The smaller the independent, the more likely it is that they specialise in a particular field: dance music, indie music, classical, even being as specific as recording only works for clarinet. Dozens of outfits are run by one person, often – literally – from their kitchen table, surrounded by boxes of Jiffy bags and chipped coffee mugs. For distribution these companies use independent distributors, which are not owned by a major, and which distribute only independent labels. Many independent labels in the UK are members of AIM (Association of Independent Music). See Useful Addresses.

THINGS YOU NEED TO KNOW

◆ Making money is a lot harder for record companies now than ever before: copyright theft in the form of internet file-sharing sites, illegal downloads, and the rocketing trend of CD-R 'burning' has been like a sharp axe striking at the tree trunk of the industry. And despite constant firefighting from the record companies, as soon as one illegal activity is clamped down upon, another leaps up. For example, when Napster was forced to go 'legal', up sprang Kazaa and Grokster. Many wonder if the way forward is to somehow work with these sites, rather than against them.

◆ Sometime in 2001/2, it finally dawned on record companies that if they couldn't beat 'em they had to join 'em, by turning new technology and the trend for downloading to their advantage. Subsequently, BMG issued the first ever commercial digital download of a single in April 2003 – Annie Lennox's 'Pavement Cracks' – and opened the floodgates for other majors to follow, via various online distributors and e-tailers (see page 21). According to BPI figures, there are now over one million tracks available on the various download services in the UK, and in the first half of 2005, 10 million legal downloads were sold – nearly twice the figure for the whole of 2004. Download figures are now included in the official singles chart, and in April 2006 Gnarls Barclay's 'Crazy' made history by getting to number one on download sales alone. Yet at time of writing, digital sales only account for about 2% of business – by 2008 this is estimated to reach 7–9%.

◆ In 2002 the US association RIAA, the Recording Industry Association of America (the equivalent of the BPI) launched lawsuits against 'major offenders' who had illegally file-shared. In 2004, the BPI decided it too would take legal action against the UK's worst offenders.

◆ There are also traditional 'pirate' CDs to contend with: the kind you buy for a couple of pounds on the beachfront in Tenerife, for example. The global sales of pirate CDs are reckoned to have more than doubled in the years from 2000–2003 to create an illegal industry worth around $4.5 billion.

◆ All of this seems to be exacerbated by the high price of CDs in the UK compared to elsewhere in the world, which averages between £10 and £16 for a new chart album. Many argue this puts CDs beyond the reach of the casual record shop browser, and yet lowering CD prices cuts record companies' profits even further. Hmm.

◆ Money is no longer made from singles. They have traditionally been seen as an 'advert for the album' and are nowadays fast becoming, in the words of one industry commentator 'a loss-making albatross', because the sales are not enough to justify the production and promotion costs. In their heyday The Beatles would have sold a million copies of a number one single. Nowadays a single might need to sell only 45,000 copies to top the charts. Record companies sometimes resort to dirty tricks like buying large amounts of a single themselves to propel it up the charts, on to *Top Of The Pops* and hopefully shift some albums on the back of it. When double CD sets like 'Now That's What I Call Music' can cram 40 hit singles on to an album for £9.99, what sensible person is going to spend their pocket money on just one of them, for £3.99? Think about it: when did you last buy a single? Fact: many record companies now make more money from mobile phone ringtones than singles.

♦ Job cuts across the record industry have been massive in the last few years, with many questioning the future viability of the way music is made and distributed to paying listeners. Could the days of the record company be numbered? It's not unthinkable.

THE DIFFERENT DEPARTMENTS WITHIN A RECORD COMPANY

A & R

A & R stands for 'Artists and Repertoire'. These are the talent spotters, the first point of contact between band/artist and record company. They find the talent, they sign it up and they handle what music they record and release. This includes choosing the right studios and producers, negotiating their fees, booking any extra session singers, musicians or 'guest stars', and taking delivery of the master tapes and so on.

A junior position would be as a scout – going to dozens of gigs, listening to dozens of tapes, talking to dozens of contacts like promoters and journalists and then persuading your boss to check out the hot new act you've just discovered. Other entry-level jobs could be A & R assistant or department co-ordinator, both of which would be more administrative, office-based jobs.

The more senior members of the team would be, in ascending order, A & R administrators, A & R managers and eventually the A & R director who has the final say on who gets signed. A & R people may only sign between one and three new acts a year – and their reputation rests on how successful these acts turn out to be.

New artists or bands are paid an 'advance' ranging from £50,000 to £500,000 or even more, on signature of their contract with a record company. The contract usually stipulates the duration of the working relationship; it could be, say, a 'two-album deal'. If the artist/band then fails to make enough money to recoup their advance they'll more than likely be dropped. If they are phenomenally successful, however, and other labels start to woo them into signing with them when their initial contract expires, the A & R department's job is to keep hold of them.

A & R is also about working with artists/bands and their managers for the duration of their career with a label – finding the best songwriters and producers for them, advising on which songs should become singles, working on their image and generally helping them make the right artistic and commercial decisions.

Marketing

Can you picture yourself talking about 'shifting more units to the Dido demographic' ? (It means selling more records to the sort of customers who buy one or two commercial, mainstream albums a year.) If so, marketing could be for you.

Marketing music is about working within an agreed budget to make customers aware of a record, and get it as high up the charts as possible. A high chart position in the week of release is vital because, for some reason, once thrown into the charts, albums act just like those sticky, rubber toy spiders you sometimes see being sold in shopping centres: you throw them as high as you can and then they crawl slowly back down again, never back up. And if they slither out of the Top 40 too quickly, albums can disappear off the public radar altogether.

Marketing also involves deciding on an artist/band's image and sleeve design; striking deals with retailers regarding in-store displays and where an album sits on the racks; writing sales notes (see below); advertising in magazines and newspapers and on the radio and TV; plus producing 'point-of-sale' material like posters, display stands, leaflets, brochures and merchandise such as badges, t-shirts, etc. Online, or digital, marketing includes building artists' websites, establishing online communities and PR.

Your compass is the 'midweeks': sneak weekday previews of Sunday's Top 40 which tell the record company how many copies of a new album have been sold so far that

Figure 3. Sales note.

week and the projected likely chart position. Marketing and sales departments act quickly on this. If an album's doing well, do they rush out some more posters to try and beat the competition to number one? If something's threatening not to enter the chart at all, should they hurriedly book more radio adverts? Or should all spend be cancelled? It's a fast-paced world and you've got to be on the ball. The plan of action around a certain release is called a '**campaign**'.

A first role would likely be marketing assistant: this would invariably involve such tasks as photocopying, ordering couriers and arranging poster displays. From marketing assistant you might eventually advance to marketing executive, marketing manager and marketing director. As you progress up the scale the job becomes more cerebral – working out long-term strategies for an artist/band and so on. What demographic are they aiming at? What image do we want them to have? The marketing world's trade magazine *Campaign* would be useful to read if you're keen on reaching this level.

Press and promotions

The press department handles enquiries from newspapers, magazines, fanzines, radio and websites about a band/artist. This includes everything from making sure reviewers have got copies of new albums, to escorting bands to Radio 1 for interviews. You'd start off as a press assistant: fielding calls, doing mail-outs and so on. Radio and TV pluggers may also be found in this department. These jobs are often farmed out to independent PR and plugging companies (go to Chapter 6 for much more detail on this field of work).

Sales

This involves dealing with record shops and persuading them to place as large an order as possible. Record company sales reps sell those products: independent labels will entrust this to an independent distributor whose briefcase will be crammed with CDs from all sorts of small labels. Sales personnel include reps and telesales staff and often work out of the distribution centre (see below). Sales reps work their way up from pounding the streets visiting small independent record stores in provincial towns and selling a couple of copies of each record, to wining and dining the head buyer of WHSmith and doing hundreds of thousands of pounds worth of business. Telesales staff hit the phones with information on new releases and try to get orders that way. Download sales may be the responsibility of an online trading manager.

Basic sales skills are essential here. As a junior rep you'll need stamina and a thick skin, and be good at closing sales and building up a reputation for reliability. If you tell a retailer the new Splodges album will sell like hotcakes and it doesn't, he's less likely to believe you next time, even when you stroll in with the new Madonna CD. A delicate mixture of blarney and brute honesty is what you'll need.

From telesales or sales rep you may, over years of hard work and lucrative results, rise to national account manager and ultimately sales director, liaising with all the big, important customers (i.e. clinking brandy glasses with Mr Woolworth at Claridges).

Production
The people responsible for the *physical* creation of the album (from the fancy artwork on the sleeve to the actual

plastic casing) are the production team. They ensure the necessary raw materials, collectively known as 'parts', i.e master tapes plus a computer disk or email of artwork, or 'films' (transparent sheets containing the artwork separated into the four colours cyan (blue), yellow, magenta and black) are to everyone's liking and make it to the manufacturing plant on schedule.

A production department will include administrators such as a production manager plus graphic designers (although sometimes record companies use freelancers working for an independent design studio).

As a junior designer, you'll need the requisite training in graphics and a flair for art. A foundation art course is a must, and a degree in graphic design is also handy.

In an administrative role you'll need organisation, a high degree of literacy and an unflappable personality. It's also handy to know a bit about CD packaging – the difference between a jewel case (the clear plastic one) and a digipack (the card one) for example.

Look out for starter jobs like production assistant, junior designer or junior product manager. (In some companies the person is charge of production is known as product manager, although confusingly this can also be the same as marketing manager.)

Classics
Usually a microcosm of its parent company, the average classics division will include one person to look after each

of the aforementioned duties. This might be a boss, marketing manager (and perhaps an assistant), press officer (and perhaps a junior), product manager and PA/coordinator, with perhaps a couple of specialist sales reps. Other staff will be shared with the rest of the company. It's no lie to say that classics people are generally several watts brighter than their pop/rock counterparts. They need to be. And as a potential junior member of staff you'll need to know the difference between John Tavener and John Taverner and that a tenor is not something you withdraw from the cashpoint.

Admin and accounts

The least glamorous area of the music biz – with apologies to record company admin and accounts people everywhere. If you're entering the music biz for fun and frolics don't reply to an ad for a facilities assistant (you'll spend all day phoning photocopy engineers and replacing lightbulbs), a post room worker (you'll spend all day in a windowless room on a franking machine) or an accounts assistant (you'll spend all day nagging people to fill in purchase order forms). Don't make the mistake of thinking these jobs will necessarily be a foot-in-the-door. Not only can these jobs be very dull, they also virtually preclude you from ever being invited to exciting launches/ parties/lunches or getting an interesting promotion into the real world of making records. (NB: Receptionists can and often do step up into more exciting roles within the company. For some reason, facilities/postroom/mainten-ance/accounts people tend to be laughed all the way to the bus stop if they try to. But maybe you can prove me wrong.)

Licensing and synchronisation ('synch')

Licensing means selling rights to use a recording to other record companies making compilations ('Ibiza Snog Choons Vol. 574' for example). As for synchronisation (or 'synch', pronounced 'sink'), ever wondered how pop songs end up on car commercials?

Synchronisation is the selling of pieces of music for use on TV shows, films, adverts, computer games, corporate videos and the like. If the producer of one of these wants to use a certain recording they must secure a license from the record company (and one from the publisher too – more in Chapter 4), usually for a fee. Licensing and synchronisation personnel liaise between the makers of such requests and the artists (via their management usually) and are a crucial and often massively profit-making department. As a first job you'd be processing license requests, inputting data and doing general admin/grunt work.

Legal/business affairs

Record company lawyers oversee all the contracts between the record company and artists, producers, publishers and numerous other factions, as well as dealing with litigation involving breach of those contracts, or intellectual property matters (such as illegal sampling). They require serious legal training before they are let loose on this tricky business so unless you have the usual law background, i.e. a law degree or conversion course, plus a year's legal practice plus a trainee period with a firm of solicitors (preferably in the entertainment division), this won't be for you just yet.

Legal secretaries are also a valued asset, so if you have experience in this line of work do consider a record company as a fun alternative to a stodgy old law firm.

International departments

All of the above refers to UK practice. The majors, however, all have international divisions based in London and housing people who oversee affiliate operations across the world, e.g. engineering an artist's break into the US or promotion across Europe, and keeping an eye on the activities of the company's headquarters around the globe.

Top tip
Only for the very bold who won't send me hate mail if it doesn't work. If you're really keen, raid your pocket money for a budget flight to Nice in January for the annual global music industry conference, Midem, held in Cannes (check ads in *Music Week* for the dates or see Useful Addresses for the contact info). Book yourself into a cheap hotel. You won't get into the conference itself unless you're a bigshot but that needn't stop you heading for the Hotel Martinez on the seafront each evening and chatting to the hundreds of record company execs who gather there after a hard day's wheeling and dealing. Helpfully, they'll probably have identity tags around their necks. They'll be at their most open and affable, i.e. six bottles of continental lager down their neck, 4 am,

miles from home, in love with the world. With a bit of luck they'll tell you everything there is to know and be an invaluable insider contact or supporter back home. Identify your target – someone your own age is best – and chat them up. They'll love it. Just don't say I sent you.

THE HIGHS AND LOWS OF WORKING FOR A RECORD COMPANY
Highs
Working for a record company is great if you like a fast-paced working environment, with snap decisions, lots of running about and few lunch breaks. For this reason it can be immensely **exciting**.

The music industry is one place where there is room for individuals: meek, conservative types will not succeed. **Strong personalities** with vision and passion will. So you're an eccentric? People think you're a little weird? Fantastic!

Few industries are as **women friendly** as this – high profile industry female figures prove this. You will encounter very little sexism or prejudicial attitudes as a woman.

Lows
On the downside, and this cannot be stressed enough, it is very **hard work**, and if you get a job with a record company you can forget ever making a 6 pm cinema date again. 'They get their pound of flesh off you' as one insider put it.

Whatever the department, the fast-moving slipstream of activity in a record company means the **pressure** is on all day long. To meet deadlines, to process information, to make decisions, to check and recheck things, to push, push, push . . . Tempers fray. People get fired. You have to keep your cool and get the job done, perfectly.

Naturally, as so many people dream of sashaying through the shiny revolving doors of a record company each morning, **competition** is fierce – not just at interview stage, but within the company itself. You are frequently reminded – both explicitly and subliminally – that in the outside world and within the building there are people who want your job.

One of the disadvantages will actually be a benefit for many: the **unsocial hours**. Even if you aren't stuck behind your desk till gone 9 pm you'll also have a duty to attend gigs, showcases and launches. Sometimes on weekends. So hobbies, sports, love-life, pets . . . something will have to give.

GETTING IN THE DOOR
See Chapter 2 for general suggestions on getting a job in the music industry.

All four majors have decent recruitment sections on their company website and it is recommended that you check these regularly.

Sony BMG: www.sonybmgmusic.co.uk/texts/jobs
Features tips on what they're looking for, how to get work experience, plus a list of current vacancies.

Universal: www.umicareers.com

Attractive website with current vacancies and details of the four year-long work placement programmes on offer. CVs need to be with the company by April, and placements start every June/July.

Warners: www.warnermusiccareers.com

Info about their three nine-month Graduate Training programmes, which can result in a real job. Also info on work experience placements.

EMI: www.emimusic.co.uk

Features a 'Search & Apply' facility for jobseekers, plus details of their paid, full-time undergraduate placements, and work experience.

So you've got that all-important interview, or work-experience placement. Now ask yourself the following:

◆ What do you know about this company's artist roster?

◆ Which are their older, established artists – and what brand new acts do they have?

◆ Do they have any albums in the Top 40 at the moment?

Top tip

Never forget that – with few exceptions – a record company's raison d'être is 'shifting units' (selling records) to raise the 'bottom line' (pure profit).

Therefore whatever job you're applying for, an employer will eye you askance if, in your interview, you can do nothing but wax lyrical about how much you enjoy one of their artists – say Johnny Splodge's bass playing on the latest Splodges' album. Express this opinion briefly by all means, but never let the interviewer think it would be more important to you than the fact the next Splodges' album has to shift x thousand copies or the finances for that quarter will be dire. Record companies are wary of 'anoraks', or die-hard fans. This is business. When albums sell badly record companies comfort themselves with lines like 'Well, we're not selling baked beans after all', but they don't really mean it. For major record companies nowadays, CDs have to be fast-moving consumer goods (FMCG) like anything else in the supermarket.

Case study 1: Elena Bello, Warner Music UK

'I had always wanted to work in the music industry. As far as training goes, I had done various courses to do with sound engineering and the music business in general, as well as a computer course. To get my first job I pestered every record label in the *Yellow Pages* with letters until one of them called me for an interview (I started at the bottom of the scale, as a receptionist). I wanted the job so desperately that I was determined to persuade them to employ me. I think I got it because they liked my determination.

'For my second job as a department co-ordinator I did a lot of research on the internet and tried to be aware of what the company was like before the interview. They also subjected us to a lot of tests (American style) that give a perfect profile of your personality and skills. By the time I got offered the job they probably knew more about me than my parents! I got the job because I got on very well with the director who interviewed me and felt at ease throughout the interview: I liked his philosophy regarding the division and expressed my genuine interest and appreciation for what he had created. I also had a pretty good track record that showed how hard-working I am and flexible towards what gets thrown at me rather than strictly sticking to my 'role'. It just so happened that the people he had in his team were rather similar to me, so I must have met the criteria he was looking for.

'I am still working in the same division (Warner Strategic Marketing) now, and I am now a marketing manager. I have gone through all the various stages to get to my current position. You certainly get a good background this way.

'I think it is getting harder and harder to get into the music business, but if this is your goal you will find a way. I think you need to be a pretty strong character if you wish to succeed. You also need to be professional, accurate, respectful (without letting people walk all over you), hard-working, enthusiastic and willing to learn, thrive under pressure, and be quite creative and flexible.

'I would definitely recommend working in a record company: I have had a great time and have met some amazing people, as well as fulfilling my all time dream.'

Case study 2: James Smith, Gut Records

'I did a degree in sociology, which was interesting for about a year, but I've always been into music and thought "What could be better than talking about music all day?". A & R jobs are very rarely advertised – they really come through word of mouth. I heard about my job through someone at Gut Records who I met randomly at a gig in Manchester, kept in contact and the rest is history. I showed a good working knowledge of music, as well as of up-and-coming bands. I had a driving license and knew my way around London so that also helped my application, because half of the job involved running/driving duties. My average week involves at least two meetings a day sandwiched in between running duties. I also spend one day a week travelling around the country looking for acts.

'Aspiring A & R scouts should be prepared to work for free, and not get much thanks for it. Get in at labels that you admire and know something about. Go to gigs, find out about unsigned bands, tell A & R people what you think's hot and what's not, and eventually someone may take notice of what you are saying.'

MANUFACTURERS

A less glitzy but crucial part of the record-making process nonetheless, manufacturers turn master tapes and art-work (i.e. 'parts') into finished products, i.e. CDs, DVDs, vinyl records or simply demo cassettes. The major record labels tend to have their own manufacturing plants at their beck and call, but all other labels turn to independent manufacturers.

The job can be hectic, as the manufacturer must get the CDs pressed and the accompanying packaging printed and assembled in time for the product to reach the distributor (see below) at least ten days before the release date. Release dates are set in stone by the time the 'parts' reach the manufacturer – which can be tricky if the record company production staff have couriered them over days later than agreed (this happens all the time!).

The production department of a record company will liaise closely with the manufacturing plant over the logistics of a chosen CD sleeve design, packaging and release dates. If a product manager at a record company decides the new Busted album should have, say, a shiny mirrored sleeve with a hologram on the disc and a free poster inside, it's up to the manufacturer to tell them how much more it will cost them to do that than stick to standard packaging, and how much longer it might take to create in the factory.

DISTRIBUTORS

Great places to get a summer job or fill-in job while you hone your CV.

When the finished CDs have been manufactured, they are delivered (or, in the industry lingo, 'shipped', regardless of the actual mode of transport) to the distributor who then sends the required number of copies on to the shops or wholesalers who've ordered them.

Distribution companies can be enormous operations comprising a giant warehouse plus back offices, and are often owned or part-owned by the major record companies. TEN and THE are two massive ones, based in Aylesbury and Newcastle-under-Lyme respectively. There are, however, dozens and dozens of independent distributors who deal with large numbers of small record labels at a time: Pinnacle and Vital are both indie label faves. But not just anyone can get their records distributed by an independent distributor: indie labels have to convince the distributor that their product is saleable and hope they will be given a distribution deal (incidentally, seeking out distribution deals in different countries is the most major and exhausting part of the small label boss's job and is what many people go to Midem for). The distributor then takes a percentage of every unit sold to a shop.

Did you know also that some major record companies will cunningly take certain releases to an indie distributor so that they can feature on the indie chart and be viewed more kindly by die-hard indie fans who might otherwise sneer at their horrible 'corporate-ness'?

The distributor's job actually starts well before the CDs are delivered to them from the manufacturer. Sales reps and telesales people within the distributor 'sell in' new releases to retailers months in advance, and are in close daily contact with the record company in-house marketing department (see also Sales above). In the front line between the record company and the retailer, the distributor's influence and importance is immense to the record company.

After a release has been in the shops for several months, the distributor will usually receive some 'returns' from retailers, i.e. copies of albums they've been unable to sell and no longer want. Returns are the bane of a distributor's (and record company's) life as they signify that a release hasn't been the sales success that was anticipated (see also Chapter 1). For a note on online distribution see page 21.

Music Publishing

In this chapter:

◆ What is music publishing?

◆ Different departments within music publishing

◆ Types of music publishing companies

◆ Getting in the door

◆ Sheet music publishers

WHAT IS MUSIC PUBLISHING?

Take a look inside the sleeve of the last CD you bought. After each track title there's probably a surname in brackets. It might be the name of the artist themselves, or someone you've never heard of. Whoever it is, they are the **songwriter**. If you're reading this chapter it's unlikely you aspire to be the penner of hits yourself, but would like to work with them – that's where the music publisher comes in.

Music publishing's golden years were in the days of Tin Pan Alley in the 1940s when famous songwriters were the pop stars of the day and their publishers would sell hundreds of printed copies of their songs for people to take home and play themselves on the piano. In those days, few artists wrote their own material, so the publishers were extremely powerful and could decide which performer should be given a particular new song first.

It's not quite like that nowadays. Music publishers still look after the songs themselves, as opposed to the artists or bands who perform them. They gather together vast catalogues of songs – by discovering, signing up and developing songwriters (or songwriting teams) or looking after catalogues of old material from artists now dead or no longer writing. Confusingly, many artists write their own songs, so they then have to sign two different deals: one with a record company as an artist and the other with a publisher as a songwriter. Today, however, cannier songwriters retain their publishing rights and set up their own little publishing arm just for themselves – there's more money in it for them this way.

The publisher pays the songwriter an advance for the song. The publisher then pays the songwriter a percentage of earnings from their music – traditionally 50 per cent – and then sells rights to record companies (to make records), sheet music publishers (to make songbooks or sell printed music over the internet) and to the makers of films and adverts (synch). Publishing companies are still powerful within the industry but are not as influential as they were in the past.

Musical copyright

The concept of 'owning' a song is a tricky one – music is just something you can hear, not a concrete object you can hold in your hand (written down it is, but sheet music is another matter, see the end of this chapter for more details). What we're talking about, when we talk about owning songs, is **copyright**. A copyright is the legal right to print, publish, perform, film or record literary, artistic or musical material. As soon as a songwriter fixes a song in tangible form – e.g. by writing it down, or just singing or playing it onto tape – it is copyrightable. It must also be original.

The difference between the copyright in a 'musical work' (the song itself, as owned by a music publisher) and a 'master sound' (e.g. a recording of that song by a band for a record company) can be a tricky concept to get your head around, but is central to the music business. The industry revolves around the buying, selling and licensing of these two rights, and the two rights are always dealt with separately (i.e. by record companies and by music publishers) because they are *not* the same thing at all.

Money from 'musical works'/songs is generated in four different ways:

1. Mechanical royalties
When a record is sold, a percentage, or royalty, goes to the publisher. This is known as **mechanical royalties**. Most music publishers are represented for issuing mechanical rights by a 'collection society' called the **MCPS** (Mechanical Copyright Protection Society).

2. Performance royalties
When a song is performed live at a concert, say, or played on the radio, this is known as **performance royalties**, and

the fees are collected by another collection society, the **PRS** (Performing Rights Society). Because keeping track of every single time a song is played on the radio or in a shop would be a bureaucratic nightmare, radio and TV stations, concert venues and shops, pubs and restaurants that play music each pay a blanket fee to the PRS for the broadcast/performance of songs from PRS's clients (virtually every publisher in possession of at least ten published or recorded works).

3. Licensing

When a producer obtains a license from the publisher to use a piece of music on a CD compilation, this is known as **licensing**. On an audio-visual production such as a TV show, film or advert, computer game or corporate video, this is known as **synchronisation**. You may remember these terms from Chapter 3 about record companies. It works in a similar way in music publishing: when a particular recording of a song (or 'a master sound recording of a musical work' to use the jargon we've just learnt) is proposed for licensing or synchronisation, the producer of the production must secure separate licenses to use the musical work (i.e. the song) and the sound recording (i.e. the recording of said song), usually for a fee. The fee is usually the same for master sound recording and musical work.

If a TV/film/advert/game producer wants to make a new recording of a song for a production they need only obtain a license from the publisher, because they become the owners of the new sound recording they have produced.

Even when rights in a musical work and master sound recording belong to the same person there are two separate contracts or one contract with two distinct parts.

Hang on in there – that's the hardest bit dealt with!

4. Sheet music
Sheet music is printed music in the form of single songs, songbooks (the 'Favourite Acoustic Guitar Songs' type of thing) or paid-for internet download (see separate section below).

(NB: There is also the issue of downloading music and generating income from MP3s – this is still in discussion among music publishers and societies everywhere.)

WHAT DO MUSIC PUBLISHERS ACTUALLY DO?

A & R/creative/promotion department
This involves:

◆ Seeking out songwriting talent. In the main they do this by receiving tip-offs from people they trust and following these up by listening to demos and attending gigs and concerts. Eventually they will sign publishing deals with songwriters. It is rare that unsolicited demos or invitations to gigs from bands result in a deal. If a deal is struck with a hot new artist who's just signed a record deal, this will generate a lot of press coverage (artists are signed up to publishing deals even if they have never written a song in their life – on the off chance they may do one day, and also to enable them to 'co-write' songs, i.e. suggest lyrics).

- Matching songwriters/composers with lyricists/librettists (if applicable).

- Getting songs used in as many places as possible: record companies, broadcasters, performers. Getting one of your writers' songs onto a big album, a Robbie Williams or Madonna album for example, would be a major coup. When artists are looking for material for a new album their record company issues a style 'brief' for potential songwriters. An A & R or creative manager will liaise between the artist's record company and the songwriter to come up with a song that will suit the artist in question and hopefully bag them a hit record.

Production/editorial department
This involves:

- Proofreading/editing/revising/rewriting music in manuscript form, then converting it into 'proper' printed sheet music by liaising with designers and printers.

- Commissioning new work and overseeing the catalogue.

Rights administration – copyright/legal/business affairs department
This deals with:

- The contractual side of publishing – drawing up agreements between publisher and songwriter.

- Licensing and synchronisation (see above).

- Registering new works with the MCPS and PRS (known collectively as the MCPS-PRS Alliance).

◆ Liaising with foreign sub-publishers and overseas collection societies so they know about new releases – it's crucial that songs are available, known of and made money from all over the world and that this is monitored in the correct fashion.

◆ Taking legal action when copyrights are infringed. This is a common occurrence in a climate where samples are so prevalent in pop music. In 2002 the rapper Dr Dre was ordered to pay $1.5 million damages after he lost a legal dispute over the use of a Fatback Band bass line on his song 'Let's Get High'. He argued that a bass line cannot be protected. He was wrong.

Sales and marketing/hire/distribution department

This is involved in the promotion and sale of printed sheet music (often a separate company – see below), as well as the hire of works to performers (e.g. a full set of 'Oklahoma' songbooks for the National Theatre production).

Accounts/royalties department

This involves a lot of number crunching, tracking the use of songs and collecting in all the money owed – dealing with the accounts departments of record companies, TV, film and advertising companies plus collection societies the MCPS and PRS. They then make payments to songwriters. In a major publishing company (or even a small one handling a famous catalogue of work) requests will stream in every day from across the world to perform or record cover versions of old songs. You can be certain the copyright manager for the Lennon/McCartney back catalogue will have earned his or her hot bath by the end of the day ('Yesterday' has been recorded about 2,000 times since 1965 and counting . . .).

KNOW YOUR SONGWRITERS

You've hopefully already heard of legendary songwriting names from the 1940s–70s like **Leiber and Stoller, Bacharach and David** and **Irving Berlin**. In addition, the names **Stock, Aitken and Waterman** (SAW) ought to ring a bell with anyone who remembers the 80s. You'll also be aware of those current artists who possess teetering mountains of their own hand-written ditties, e.g. **Paul McCartney**.

But here are a few more names that you would do well to be aware of if seeking a job in this arena – celebrated, contemporary songwriters who have written some of the biggest hits of the last few years.

Diane Warren – the diva's fave and American queen of the schmaltzy, big-budget love ballad.

Brian Rawling (and his company Xenomania) – the only songwriter named in *Music Week*'s 'Most Influential People in UK Music' and responsible for hits by Enrique Inglesias and Cher.

Cathy Dennis – eighties UK pop singer turned songwriter, who arguably made Kylie a megastar with 'Can't Get You Out Of My Head' and writes pop hits for numerous artists.

Brian Higgins – this UK writer has written hits for Girls Aloud amongst others.

Steve Robson – UK songwriter who has successfully broken through both here and across the Atlantic with acts including Westlife, Atomic Kitten, Busted and Wynonna Judd.

Read the songwriting credits on your records or on the *Music Week* weekly charts. Are there any names that keep cropping up?

DIFFERENT TYPES OF MUSIC PUBLISHING COMPANIES

Majors: Warner Chappell, EMI, BMG, Universal, Sony/ ATV (see Useful Addresses).

Independents: there are hundreds, some of the best-known including Windswept, Chrysalis, Carlin, Boosey and Hawkes, Mute Song, Notting Hill, Big Life, Minder and IMG.

Writer-publishers: these are famous songwriters who don't need a publisher to represent them because they are so famous that record companies come begging to them.

There are specialist publishers for every genre of music you can imagine. Obviously the company ethos and office vibe will differ from one to another, so do your research.

THE HIGHS AND LOWS OF WORKING IN MUSIC PUBLISHING

Highs

Publishing is the more 'academic' side of the music industry, and as such hugely rewarding to anyone fascinated by the idea of intellectual property and/or the art of songcraft. A friendlier, more welcoming atmosphere tends to prevail here than in many other areas.

Lows

Long hours, stress and often brain-numbing tedium at the lower levels. And sadly, while the experience, knowledge and friendships earned in entry-level publishing jobs are priceless, the pay is peanuts – as little as £13k in some cases – resulting in many young people in the field doing extra jobs just to keep themselves clothed and able to pay their mobile phone bill . . .

GETTING IN THE DOOR

See Chapter 2 for further suggestions on getting a job.

An invaluable resource to anyone interested in music publishing, the UK **Music Publishers' Association (MPA)** operates a useful website (**www.mpaonline.org.uk**) which also operates a Jobseekers' List which is circulated to MPA members (i.e. publishing houses) for recruitment purposes. Enter your details online and keep your fingers crossed.

The good news is that the MCPS, PRS and MPA are all excellent places to begin a career in music publishing and many who are now in top jobs began their working lives toiling here. There are many entry-level positions within the MCPS-PRS Alliance and jobs in these organisations are like an education in themselves, to the extent that one music publisher has dubbed the Alliance a 'recruitment pool'. Time spent working at the MCPS-PRS Alliance is a very valuable asset to have on a CV, providing you with a definite advantage over other candidates.

So a great way to start would be to send a CV and covering letter to the human resources departments of these organisations requesting information about job vacancies or work placements.

An entry-level job might be something like a copyright clerk at the MCPS – receiving song registration sheets and cross-referencing and updating the database. A similar job at the PRS might involve assessing live events or broadcast works, categorising the events/shows/trans-missions and inputting them on the PRS database to be cross-referenced with sample dates, song info, info from overseas, etc.

Once you get a foot in the door at these organisations it's easy to move up within the company. They are 'investors in people' and you are constantly being offered classes to sharpen your skills and improve your knowledge, and make you more employable when you are ready to move on to a publishing company. If you can make it through the initial tedious role, then the second job you get (within the company or not) will be more challenging, with more lateral thinking and artist/publisher liaison.

Top tip
You don't have to have a PhD in musicology or spend every weekend writing killer verses, choruses and bridges yourself in order to work in music publishing, but an understanding of and feel for the mechanics of song construction will impress

employers and show you're serious. Music publishers tend to be a rather more sober and academic bunch than other music industry bods – the word 'fogeyish' springs to mind in certain cases. But this is because they care deeply about their subject. So gen up: Tim De Lisle's *Lives Of The Great Songs* (Pavilion) is great for nuggets like how the Rodgers and Hart song 'My Funny Valentine' shares a crucial compositional device with the nursery rhyme 'Three Blind Mice'. So now you know.

Case study: Angela Penhaligon, Mute Song

'I have always known that I wanted to be involved with music as a career but I was too practical to say, "When I grow up, I wanna be a rock star" so was grateful for the security of a day job when it came along. Having studied music from the age of four all the way through university, it just seemed natural to work in the field of music in some capacity.

'My first music industry job in the UK was through a temp agency as a copyright clerk at the MCPS – it wasn't glamorous and it certainly wasn't what I had in mind. I was drawn to it initially because it had something to do with music, and the issue of intellectual property always interested me. Being a copyrighter was a bit like being a glorified data inputter, there was the odd occasion where I'd help an artist with their forms or resolve a sample clearance, or deal with the foreign societies; that was a bit more interesting.

'When I left that job I realised I had actually learned a lot more than I thought and I made a fair few friends who'd moved on to do similar jobs to what I do now – they were useful contacts, and we still help each other out now when we can. While working at the MCPS I started writing a column for a website that specialised in music outside of the norm – it was a great way to stay in touch with what's happening in new music while doing the nine-to-five thing.

'I then went to work at PRS in member services. This was great experience because answering people's questions is the best way to learn, and the queries were always varied and required research. The pay was peanuts, so I promoted gigs in Camden and played in a band to make extra money on the side. I then went to do royalties for the BBC, which was horrible – I was over-worked, constantly facing impossible deadlines, departmental morale was at a real low. I had to get out, so applied for the Mute Song job advertised at the back of *Music Week*. They were specifically looking for someone with experience at both MCPS and PRS, and my extra activities outside work was what set me apart from the other applicants (I'm told), because it showed a passion for what I do and why I do it. That passion interested them as much as having the relevant experience.

'I am now a music publishing assistant at Mute Song. Because there are only five of us, we all have to do a bit of everything. I do a lot of artist liaison, helping them with their queries, I am A & R coordinator, I assist the general manager, do a bit of royalty inputting which is a bit like data inputting twice a year, and register new tracks. I also keep in touch with our foreign sub-publishers, assist with licensing tracks for film and television, do mail-outs of new products – there's never a dull moment.

'I love feeling like I'm helping the artist. I enjoy A & R-ing a new and exciting band, but I hate writing rejection letters to the hundreds of people that send us their material so I try to make it as polite as possible.

'As for the kind of person you need to be, I think one needs to find music publishing interesting in the first place. If the idea of copyright or licensing sounds painfully dull, don't go into publishing. The A & R bits are fun, taking bands out to dinner and going to record launch parties – that's good too, but the majority of the job is not about that stuff. A genuine interest in music and caring about the artists you work with is important, too. One should have an inquisitive mind and enjoy investigating things; you need to do a lot of lateral thinking and understand relationships within the music industry.

'It's hard to get a job at a music publisher straight away, so be willing to do some of the grunt work, bide your time, learn about how the bureaucratic cogs of the publishing industry work, because the knowledge will come in handy later.'

SHEET MUSIC PUBLISHERS

Another source of income to the music publisher, and the songwriters they represent, is in printed music, or 'sheet music'. Back in the days of Tin Pan Alley, music publishing was not just about matching performers and songwriters for the purpose of records, but also very much about sheet music. Now the sheet music aspect has dwindled and publishing's more a question of copyrights, synchs and intellectual property.

Nonetheless, music publishers continue to strike deals with sheet music publishers who then are granted limited rights to make sheet music products for them: i.e. the music written out in a stave with bars, treble clefs, etc. and sold to people like your 11-year-old niece for her piano lessons, or your Uncle Len for his blues cover band. You can buy single songs or whole songbooks.

The two biggest sheet music publishers are International Music Publications (IMP) and Music Sales (see Useful Addresses). Jobs within these companies range from production/editorial (see above) to publisher relations (persuading music publishers to let you print sheet music for them) and sales/marketing.

Increasingly, sheet music is available over the internet, as paid-for downloads (e.g. **www.sheetmusicdirect.com**) so this might be another area worth considering.

Music PR and Plugging

In this chapter:

◆ What is music PR and plugging?

◆ Highs and lows

◆ Getting in the door

◆ Radio/TV pluggers

WHAT IS MUSIC PR AND PLUGGING?

PR stands for '**public relations**'. How does a musician relate to the public? Through their music, yes, but also through the media. In other words: the press, internet, radio and TV. A record company press officer or music PR company deals with a band/artist's relationship with the first two: the press, also known as 'print media' and relevant websites, e.g. Drowned in Sound, or Yahoo! Launch. (The mechanics of getting an act on radio or TV is a specialised field in itself, known as **plugging**, and is done either in-house by a record company or via a specialist agency. This is dealt with at the end of this chapter.)

PR is essential to an artist's success. Obviously, the artist's talent is vital too, but the sheer volume of talented-yet-unknown acts out there proves it is not enough in this tough industry. Good PR – in the form of favourable reviews, interviews, photos and mentions – can make or break a record, tour, or new act. And, crucially, record companies are all too aware that a full-page interview with a photo costs nothing (bar the PR's fee) and is a thousand times more effective than paying for the same size advert in the same magazine: after all, who takes adverts seriously?

WHAT DO MUSIC PR COMPANIES DO?

Music PR companies are hired by record companies or directly by artists themselves. They are asked to generate press coverage for a particular artist's albums, singles, concerts, and very occasionally non-musical events such as political activity or books. (Some artists are handled in-house by their record company's in-house press office – see Chapter 3.) This can mean anything from getting their act onto the front cover of a national magazine, right down to a small album review on page 37 of the *Bristol Evening Post* and even includes fleeting mentions in gossip columns that might not have anything whatso-ever to do with music! Whenever you read something about music in the press you can be sure that, somewhere along the way, a music PR was involved.

♦ A music PR's first duty is to assemble and keep up-to-date the widest, most detailed bank of **informa-tion** possible on the people they need to target: i.e. **journalists and editors** of music magazines, the arts/ music pages of newspapers and magazines, as well as freelance journalists and relevant music websites. They need to know these people on a first-name basis, and have some idea of their likes, dislikes and the general editorial policy of their publication. They must also keep track of staff changes.

◆ They work out **where best to concentrate their efforts** for the particular album, single, concert or other project they have been asked to publicise. Which publications will be most interested in this band or artist? Which will probably hate it? The saying 'all publicity is good publicity' is bunkum when it comes to music PR. A scathing review can sometimes get the music PR into big trouble . . .

◆ They will then send out a **press release** (an A4 sheet – sometimes longer – containing punchy, persuasive information about the artists and the album), a **biography** (information on the band, how they met, where they are from, their past work, etc.) and a **'promo' CD** if publicising a record (usually in a plain plastic sleeve) several weeks before it is released. A week or two later they follow it up with phone calls, emails and perhaps the odd attempted bribe (lunch, a drink, a trip abroad to meet the band if the journalist promises to write something, although this is increasingly frowned upon, to the chagrin of many journalists!), all pushing for a mention in print of their band/artist.

◆ They also organise **guest lists** for concerts – and if it's a hot ticket they'll be so inundated with requests they have to be selective.

◆ If press activity is generated, the PR **oversees** it all. This means escorting the artists to the journalists, or vice versa, organising any travel and seeing to everyone's needs from pounding the streets for the particular type of sandwich the artist wants (a PR I know once ran around the whole of Soho looking for a poached salmon sandwich for a classical composer she was looking after) to buying the journalist a drink while they wait around.

◆ They then collate any press coverage and present it in a **report** to the record company. After this they are the go-between between journalists and artists for any follow-up matters or general enquiries.

◆ An independent PR agency will often also be involved in their own **A & R** (see Chapter 3 if you need a reminder of what this term means): seeking out good, unknown bands through demos they are sent, by attending gigs and through their contacts within the industry. They then approach and offer to represent hot new bands who are looking for a record label – this way they are on board from the beginning.

◆ Frequently, good PRs are consulted by the record company on **A & R decisions** such as which single from an album would be the best one to release, what the release date should be, and when and where gigs should take place.

◆ They also organise **promotional photo sessions** for bands: booking studios, sourcing photographers and so on.

◆ There is often someone on the team, usually a junior, who specialises in **regional press**: dealing with local newspapers and listings magazines and so on. This person often services student publications as well.

in-house press

Artist:	**The Innocence Mission**
Title:	*Befriended*
Cat Number:	**AGN010LP/AGN010CD**
Release Date:	**24th November 2003**

Track Listing: 1) tomorrow on the runway
2) when mac was swimming
3) I never you from the sun
4) beautiful change
5) martha avenue love song
6) one for sorrow, two for joy
7) no storms come
8) sweep down early
9) walking around
10) look for me as you go by

The Innocence Mission began as four friends who met during a Catholic high school production of the musical Godspell. Since their fortuitous parochial meeting, they have released five critically acclaimed albums: *The Innocence Mission* (*A&M* 1989), *Umbrella* (*A&M* 1991), *Glow* (*A&M* 1995), *Birds Of My Neighborhood* (*RCA* 1999) and *Small Planes* (*W.A.R.* 2001). Although they remain friends, the one consistent incarnation of The Innocence Mission revolves around the inspired musical (and literal) marriage of guitarist Don Peris and his wife, vocalist/pianist Karen Peris.

Arguably their best work to date, their new album, *Befriended*, is a haunting collection of 10 songs that features the interplay of Don's gorgeously warm and shimmering electric guitars with Karen's transcendently lovely vocals and moving lyrics. Often earmarked as the group's most recognisable sound, Karen's voice is a thing of wonder yet at the same time, has a familiar comfort to it, not unlike a beloved mother singing a lullaby to an adoring child. On *Befriended,* the influences of folk-legends like Simon and Garfunkel and Fairport Convention are evident, as are The Sundays & Hope Sandoval, yet The Innocence Mission carve out a sound, at once melancholic and joyful, that is all their own. One prescient type summed it up thus, *'think of an American Astrud Gilberto making a record with Buffalo Springfield'.* You begin to get the picture - right?

Press for Previous Releases:

'[The Innocence Mission] have delivered a record as sad and yet beautiful as anything that has been produced in years. Simply brilliant.' - **Rolling Stone.com**
'Of all the new singer-songwriters, Karen Peris is the most interesting to me.' **Joni Mitchell**

And what of their singularly un-hip name? As Karen puts it, *'(it) was the idea that music can be a shelter, and music is something that is made with pure joy, with purity of intention, purity of heart'.*

If you as a listener have one, a heart that is, there is absolutely no way that you will not succumb to the charms and depths of this record. Easily one of 2003's finest.

Further information, interviews & pics from:

'a cottage industry'

vat reg. no. 768030820   company reg. no. 4504545

Figure 4. A music PR company press release.

A typical day in the life of a junior music PR

10 am   Arrive in office. Go through the day's newspapers and magazines for articles on your company's bands/artists.

11 am   Photocopy and file the above.

12 noon   Meeting to discuss the upcoming press campaign for The Splodges' new album.

1 pm   Quick sandwich while listening to the new Splodges' album on headphones.

2 pm   Draft press release and biography to accompany new Splodges' album.

4 pm   Phone as many regional music editors and journalists as possible to see if they received the DJ Dave CD you sent them last week and what they thought of it. Make notes.

6 pm   Fix the paper jam in the photocopier and make everyone coffee.

8 pm   Head to Dog & Frog pub with colleagues to meet journalists invited to watch a performance by new, young singer-songwriter Sandy Sad, who your company represents.

12 midnight   Fall into bed, listening to Rob da Bank on the radio . . .

DIFFERENT TYPES OF MUSIC PR COMPANIES

No surprises here. There are big companies and small ones. Many household name bands and artists are with big PR companies like MBC (Madonna, Dido and others), Coalition or Hall Or Nothing, but it does not necessarily follow that small companies never handle any major clients. You see, bigger does not necessarily mean better. A small company, perhaps with only two or three staff but a warm, efficient approach, can generate an awful lot of goodwill and column inches, while a bigger (perhaps bossier) one can find its loftiness actually backfires, aggrieving journalists and creating bad press. Smaller PR companies with great reputations and usually smaller, more 'niche' artists include Hermana, Stone Immaculate and ID Publicity. Furthermore, allegiances are notoriously fickle in this area – bands have been known to switch PR company with each new album. There are also dedicated online and regional PR companies.

THE HIGHS AND LOWS OF WORKING IN MUSIC PR

Highs

First the good news. An experienced PR can enjoy a great deal of travel. If you work on American bands, for example, you may find yourself flying to the Big Apple every month. You'll enjoy the satisfaction that comes with seeing your band on the cover of NME and knowing it was down to you. And yes, let's face it, you could spend a lot of time at awards ceremonies, glamorous record launches and backstage parties. Which ought to make everything in the next paragraph worthwhile . . .

Lows

Now for the bad news. When celebrities talk about their publicists it's easy to imagine that all who work in the music PR world spend all their time eating expensive lunches, fighting off paparazzi and jetting off to LA. Not true. The work can – especially for someone starting out – be boring, difficult and not remotely glam.

You need to be diplomatic, thick-skinned and patient all day long. Musicians and journalists must be two of the most stubborn and elusive types of people there are, and lucky old you will be dealing with both! Bear in mind that often a band or artist will just want to concentrate on the music and let it speak for itself: it is their contract with the record company that obliges them to jump through various press and promotional hoops. They can, on occasion, be difficult. Journalists can be impossible to get hold of – you'll speak to their voicemail more than to them – and rude and unhelpful when you do reach them. Many PRs would say dealing with journalists is the part of their job they hate the most!

Being so crucial to an artist's success or failure, fame or famine, you won't be surprised to hear that enormous pressure is exerted on PRs to develop to the max the public image of their artists, especially if large sums of money have been invested. If a PR doesn't deliver they will not be given any more work for that artist. Sometimes it can feel as if the whole world is against them . . .

GETTING IN THE DOOR

See Chapter 2 for further suggestions on getting a job.

An entry-level job will normally be as a junior PR, or office junior, doing pretty menial work: press cuttings, photocopying, envelope-stuffing, taxi-ordering, post, etc. After some time you would begin to do some regional press. From this you can rise to being a proper PR with decent acts to oversee and a lot more travel and fun. With enough experience under their belts some PRs eventually set up their own company, work exclusively for one artist as their personal publicist or manager, or take up a better paid, in-house senior role within a record company.

Consider the following:

◆ Do you really have the right sort of personality to be a PR? It sounds rather blunt, unkind and prejudiced, but music PR is a field in which a plummy accent, smart suit and clean shoes won't do you many favours, nor necessarily will excellent educational qualifications. Most music PRs rate the right sort of personality much, much higher than any of these. Are you the sort of person who feels at home in pubs and clubs, can stay up late – but still get up for work the next day? Do you find it easy to talk to people and make friends? Could you talk favourite cocktails with a journalist one minute, and break up a fight between a member of a rock band and a passer-by (believe me, it has happened!) the next?

◆ When applying to a PR company, check which artists the company looks after. Make sure you know a handful and have an opinion on them. Go and see a few of them live or buy their albums. Do they have a unique selling-point? Perhaps they met in prison, are Icelandic, or a brother-and-sister act, or have a particularly distinctive vocalist. How would you try to convince a journalist to do a feature about them?

♦ Familiarise yourself with the main music press: specialist magazines like *Q*, *Mojo*, *Uncut*, *Muzik*, *Smash Hits* and *NME* plus the music sections of the main newspapers. See how different they are in their likes and dislikes, their style, the amount of coverage they give to music. For example, would the *Daily Mirror* be likely to do a two-page spread on a little-known American heavy-metal band? Would *Mojo* ever wax lyrical over Dannii Minogue?

♦ Be cool. What I mean by this is: don't let them think you'd act star-struck when faced with an artist. Be professional and down-to-earth. The employer will want to be able eventually to entrust you with looking after an artist all day – eating, drinking, travelling with them, seeing them at their jetlagged, hungover worst – and know you won't be asking for an autograph for Aunty Glenda, or acting like a 13-year-old schoolgirl/ boy face-to-face with Gareth Gates. Even the man who escorts Kylie around all day is expected to stay cool. And that can't be easy, can it?

Top tip
Find out the names of a few key pop writers by looking in the major newspapers and magazines and drop them into conversation in an interview. A

killer answer to a question on how you'd try to obtain press coverage for a new UK garage group would be something like this (fictional names and publications of course!): 'Well, I know that Clarence Pilkington-Smith of the *Daily Whinge* really hates urban music so I probably wouldn't waste too much time on him, but I noticed Suzie Smith of the *Observograph* wrote something nice about UK garage the other week, so I think there's a reasonable chance she'd at least do a review, if not a feature'.

Case study: Alison Millar, age 21, Hermana PR, London

'After my A-levels at 18, I went straight to Buckinghamshire Chilterns University College in High Wycombe, to study music industry management and marketing. I started working at Hermana while I was there. I knew that if I wanted to get a job in music I'd have to get a bit of work experience behind me, so I sent my CV off to loads of companies. Hermana PR got back to me after my CV was passed on to them by another company I'd been contacting about work experience. I came in on my days off uni and did mailouts, photocopying, regional press and other bits and bobs. I did that for most of my three-year course. When I graduated in the summer of 2002 I was lucky enough to be offered a full-time job with the company! Now I do all the regional and student press – both on releases and when someone plays shows around the country. As well as that there are mailouts to be done and other jobs such as photocopying and filing. I guess I always wanted to work in music. As a teenager I spent all my money on gig tickets or CDs. I stumbled across the music industry management course by accident and thought it sounded better than doing a geography degree! I got a lot out of my degree – learning about marketing and the music business as a whole, but it's nothing without actual practical experience. I think the most important qualities a music PR needs are organisation and passion. We're a small company and deal with a massive amount of artists, including the Yeah Yeah Yeahs and Josh Rouse, so you've got to be on the ball knowing who's doing what and when.'

RADIO AND TV PLUGGERS

Pluggers do basically the same job as a press officer but for TV and radio instead of newspapers and magazines. They are employed by record companies to get records played by broadcasters of all sorts: from small, local radio stations to *CD:UK*. Pluggers are often in-house with a record company, but if not, a record company will outsource the work to a company such as Anglo Plugging, Absolute or LD Promotions.

Their role is important not only to the record companies – because a presence in the public eye and ear sells records – but also because broadcasters, whatever their audience, need to be kept up-to-date on the new releases so they can keep their schedules fresh and interesting.

A radio plugger's job involves persuading radio stations to play their records and interview their artists. They visit radio stations in person, lugging around all the releases they are trying to plug. If an artist has been booked for an interview or live session they accompany them.

The lists of songs a radio station plans to play over the course of a week is known as the 'play list'. This is subdivided into A-list, B-list and C-list. A good song that's on lots of radio A-lists can garner up to 3,000 airings a week across the UK. For the radio plugger, the climax of the week comes on Thursday morning when Radio 1's playlist is published, although the other radio stations' playlists are also seized upon.

US artists and bands are outnumbering British acts when it comes to radio play, about 70:30 in favour of US acts. In Australia, France and Canada there are government quota systems in place to ensure plenty of home-grown talent gets played, and therefore purchased. Over here, radio stations – Radio 1 in particular – have been criticised for not playing enough British talent. But many insist the onus is on the record company to come up with great songs that can compete with the best US hits.

A TV plugger's job is along the same lines, but with television: trying to get music and artists on relevant TV programmes. They deal with TV producers and band bookers (if it's a show with a live music element such as *This Morning*, for example) and have an easier job if the song they are plugging has already been well-received by radio.

$$6$$

Artist Managers

In this chapter:

- What is an artist manager?
- What do they do?
- Getting in the door

WHAT IS AN ARTIST MANAGER?

Bob Marley's took five bullets in the groin for him. Beyoncé Knowles's is her father and Celine Dion's her husband. Former Australian prime minister Paul Keating used to be one. The most crucial relationship in an artist's working life (after their pet Pomeranian, of course) is with their manager. Artist managers work directly for the artist or band, and are their chief representative/ally/ defender/punchbag when it comes to everyone that can help them become a star: i.e. the record company, the publisher, the concert promoter (basically every other person in this book). See how, in the diagram in Chapter 1 (page 7), the manager literally surrounds and encloses the artists like a buffer.

Managers try to ensure artists are left free to concentrate on what they do best: music. *And* ensure they don't have to do anything so demeaning as picking up a ringing phone all by themselves . . .

In return they get 15 to 25 per cent of their artists' income – usually 20 per cent, although this isn't set in stone.

The hours average 10 am to 6 pm but be prepared for them to inevitably run into the wee small hours.

WHAT DO ARTIST MANAGERS DO?

Everything, really – that's the simple answer. Managers literally 'look after' their client. Why else do so many singers end up being managed by their own mother? Managers do everything including:

◆ negotiating record company contracts

◆ negotiating publishing deals

◆ liaising with merchandisers

◆ liaising with PR companies or record company press officers and pluggers

◆ dealing with booking agents

◆ dealing with the relevant overseas companies

◆ handling the legal side and appointing a lawyer

◆ handling accountancy, maybe appointing an accountant

◆ appointing tour managers

. . . and much more.

So one day you might be acting tough with the record company lawyer over paragraph three clause four, the next urging your artist to smile more at a magazine photo shoot. One day ringing the accountant about the tax return, the next ordering the Chinese takeaway. If an artist can't get out of bed in the morning to do promotional duties for the new album it's the manager's job to haul their charge onto their feet, order room service and placate the anxious record company exec outside the door who is at risk of bursting a bloodvessel as she has 20 journalists waiting impatiently in the hotel lobby downstairs. The most devoted/foolhardy (delete as applicable) artist manager may even end up performing duties such as mortgage applications and dog walking. It's that diverse.

But it's also a little more romantic than that. When everyone else is trying to turn their artist into something they're not, the manager can be the only one defending their integrity and struggling to maintain what was so special about them in the first place. Managers will urge the record company to take a long-term view of their client as opposed to the fast buck short-termism of many record company suits. So if the manager feels their artist is being exploited (say inappropriate photos that dramatically alter their public image) or neglected (say a meagre marketing budget for their new record) they'll fight their corner.

SOME FAMOUS BRITISH MANAGERS

Simon Fuller and his company 19 Management – famous for the Spice Girls, S Club 7 and the 'Pop Idol' concept which has netted gazillions. A modern legend.

Louis Walsh – familiar from 'Pop Idol' this veteran has mothered Boyzone, Westlife and Girls Aloud.

Peter Leak and Network Management – Dido, Avril Lavigne and Coldplay are some of the big names whose hands these folks hold through the peaks and troughs of stardom.

Colin Lester and Ian McAndrew and their company Wildlife – much-envied hotshot managers of Craig David, Travis and more.

Chris Morrison of CMO Management – a veteran who's worked with Thin Lizzy, Ultravox, (Nigel) Kennedy, Blur, Morcheeba, Turin Brakes and many others.

David Enthoven and IE Music – much-respected and very busy chaperones of one Mr Robbie Williams and formerly bands such as Roxy Music.

GETTING IN THE DOOR

Management companies are firms that represent several artists at the same time. Whether you want to learn the business through a big, comforting corporate structure or fly solo, the same principles apply when it comes to knocking on doors. (See also Chapter 2 for more general advice on getting in through the corporate route.)

Most managers opt for the life they lead because they find an artist or band they long to manage. They might have no actual experience – just a firm belief they can make this artist a success – and end up learning on the job. So next time you're in your local toilet venue being blown away by a fantastic band, buy them a drink afterwards and ask them if they need a manager (obviously this wouldn't work with U2 but it might with a local or college band, or anyone with talent and aspirations that reach beyond a bi-annual pub gig).

Do you have what it takes? Have you got a thick skin, persistence, patience, tolerance, sense of humour and a rudimentary knowledge of the principles of management and business? Maybe you were entertainments officer or social secretary at college, organised gigs in the student bar or roadied for a friend's band. It's all great experience.

The most essential requirement is absolute faith in your client: if you don't believe they're the best thing since sliced bread you will never persuade anyone else they are.

Top tip
In return for a discounted membership fee of £80 per annum (correct at time of going to print) the Music Managers Forum (MMF) will open its doors to anyone interested in music management, regardless of age, experience or level. With the emphasis firmly on information-sharing and networking, its activities include monthly masterclasses in London and Manchester (planned for other big cities in the near future) where you will meet, and get the chance to chat up, potential employers and hear

about vacancies, or, if you wish to set up your own business as a manager, brain-pick and make friends. There are also bi-annual open days and more informal monthly 'surgeries' where you can have a pint and talk foreign sub-publishing advances to your heart's content.

Courses

The University of Westminster is one institution that offers a degree in Commercial Music which covers music management. Check the BPI website for up-to-date info on others.

Books

The MMF (see above) publish the trade magazine *MM Forum* and a specialist manual, *The MMF Guide to Professional Music Management*, both of which will come in handy if you're serious about this line of work.

Many managers start out as roadies, become tour managers (see Chapter 7) and work their way up. Or they may have a background as musicians or producers themselves and find that the business angle eventually lures them in.

Case study: Mark Vernon, Firebrand Management

'Managers are like lone wolves in this business – they tend to be self-employed and are therefore open to all the elements. There's a huge protection zone around artists and record companies, and artist managers have to be ready to be the first over the top and be prepared to get into the firing line with all concerned.

'Initially I wanted to be a musician so I formed a band. However, with no money coming in this meant having to do a variety of jobs – working in HMV, on building sites, a stint in a French supermarket (to learn French). Eventually I became a confectionery rep for a while . . . which at least brought in a secure wage, but more importantly the freedom not to be constrained by working nine-to-five, and therefore time to rehearse and perform plus the company car that meant I could get the band and gear to and from gigs!

'Throughout this period I was always writing music and in 1985 I had saved enough to quit my job for a year or so and plunge into being a songwriter and focussing on the band. I chose to manage myself and ended up signing a publishing deal, going on to record an album with John Cale producing, and then negotiating licensing deals for the album in the UK and Europe. Looking back on it, I think I would have benefited from approaching a separate management company and concentrating on making the music, but at the time it was probably my experience as a sales rep that gave me the confidence to get in touch with Cale's manager in the first place. I had always been taught 'if you don't ask you don't get'.

[*Various members of his group (Rob Ellis and Ian Oliver) with him as manager, ended up backing PJ Harvey. His plan was to move more into production and subsequently he ended up producing PJ's first single 'Dress' and co-producing 'Happy and Bleeding' off her first album 'Dry' in 1992. Due to the increasing amount of business activity this led to him becoming her manager.*]

'I set up my own company, Firebrand Management, in 1991. Since then and up until the present I have tended to specialise in representing the careers of more 'cutting edge' artists such as Gorky's Zygotic Mynci, BJ Cole, Trash Palace and, in a curious loop of circumstances, John Cale.

'Watching your artist play a sell-out show to an enthusiastic audience and knowing afterwards that they are actually happy with the performance is a real high point of the job, as is reading a constructive and positive review, and seeing your artist on the cover of a magazine. Also getting the deal signed and celebrating, but be warned: only once the cheque has cleared! Seeing your artist attain a favourable chart position and hearing them on the radio or seeing them on TV whilst knowing they've achieved this without having had to make creative sacrifices is a real pleasure. I also enjoy the travelling – it's not an office-orientated job, it's unpredictable and that feeds the adrenalin and keeps you alert.

'The minus points are people saying they'll do something and not doing it. In terms of dealing with people you need an ability to separate the good guys from the bad and knowing the difference will go some way towards protecting your artist from the latter. Perhaps the most unsavoury side of the business is litigation and going to court. It has been jokingly suggested 'where there's a hit there's a writ' but in reality this is tiresome, stressful and horrifically expensive. I have always ended up on the winning side but my advice would be wherever possible to try to settle matters amicably and move on with dignity intact.

'To succeed as an artist manager in the music business you need energy, initiative, team leadership and team building, foresight, creativity, patience, tolerance, dependability, responsibility, consistency, tenacity, decisiveness, occasional bloody-mindedness, strength and vision . . . and at all times. Above all, you need the ability to build up a close relationship of trust with the artist by supplying them with a solid and reliable support mechanism whilst retaining a sense of perspective and humour. Knowing a foreign language can also really help when you are dealing with overseas business contacts.

'Try to get work experience at a management company, but research them first – they'll be more favourably disposed if you know what kind of artists they represent and a little about the history of the management company rather than going in blind. My assistant has been with me for the last six years. When she sent in her CV, it was clear we had compatible taste in music and that beyond that she had a good working knowledge of artists on my roster. This, allied to a diligent and proactive outlook, helped her get the job. Initially I started off by giving her small things to do as work experience, but over the years I have built up sufficient trust in her and her experience that I know the company is in dependable hands should I need to be away.

'In terms of CV I'm not necessarily impressed when I see someone's done media studies as a degree or done some particular music business course. Apart from basic computer literacy I'm far more interested in the personality and seeing what kind of music they're into than pages of qualifications. The sorts of questions I ask myself: Can I have a good conversation with that person? Have they got energy and enthusiasm? Are they reliable? Have they got a sense of humour? Can they cope with the unpredictable hours and pressures that the job will entail? Do they want to learn? Will they get on with the artist? Above all, have they got a good work ethic or are they just in it for the ride?

'There is no hard and fast rule that says you have to be in the music business already to be a good manager. It takes more than just swotting up, academic qualifications or interest in music – you've got to have the right temperament. As well as believing in your artist and the music, if you're a dependable, organised and outgoing personality it will help you to do well and be able to sell yourself as a person (and therefore your artist) to others.'

Top tip
Check out **www.bandreg.com** to see if that talented but manager-less band you hope to look after share their name with anyone else, and gen up on the international rules and regulations surrounding band names. This ought to kick off an interesting discussion on band names (and these can go on for

hours, days, years even) when you sidle up to them after a gig for an informal chat. With a bit of luck they'll be so impressed by your knowledge, foresight and sturdy, calm managerial skills they'll be begging you to tie their shoelaces for them by last orders.

7

Live Music: Booking Agents, Concert Promoters, Tour Managers and Roadies

In this chapter:

- ◆ The live music scene

- ◆ Highs and lows

- ◆ What booking agents do

- ◆ What promoters do

- ◆ What tour managers do

- ◆ Roadies

The UK live music scene's heyday was in the 1960s and 70s when legendary svengali Larry Parnes brought US acts over and every town had its own concert hall. But times changed and the rise in accessibility of home entertainment like videos and computer games in the 1980s took a big chunk out of this industry sector. Nowadays the gig-goer is lucky if a major rock star's so-called 'UK tour' takes in more than just London, Manchester and Birmingham.

And yet today the UK live music scene is in robust health, with major music festivals now as much a part of the national calendar as Wimbledon (Glastonbury tickets in particular selling out within nanoseconds), a rise in so-called 'boutique festivals' such as The Big Chill and All Tomorrow's Parties, and the now-habitual phenomenon of unsigned but hotly-tipped bands selling out London venues before even inking a record deal. A new generation of guitar-music-loving gig-goers are swarming into live gigs. And importantly the live music industry has one big benefit that the record companies don't – it offers an experience they can't burn from their friends or blag for free off the internet.

Not all tours 'break even' (make enough money to cover costs) for the record company, but they nonetheless remain an essential part of the marketing strategy, keeping the band in the public eye and satisfying the fans. A healthy live music scene is to the advantage of virtually everyone in the music industry, creating not only a healthy revenue stream in its own right but also boosting sales of albums, videos and DVDs, posters, books, magazines, souvenir underpants, the lot.

THE HIGHS AND LOWS OF WORKING IN THE LIVE MUSIC ARENA

Highs

As much live music as you can handle plus the chance to be at music's grass-roots level – a very exciting place to be and often a lot more 'real' than the recording side of the industry.

Lows

Late nights, long hours, jet lag, artistic tantrums, last-minute disasters in front of thousands, and a very thin line between making it worthwhile and people losing money and face.

BOOKING AGENTS

What is a booking agent?

A music booking agent handles a band/artist's live performances and tours at home and abroad. The agent works with the manager (and the record company if applicable) to guide them on the best venues, towns, duration of the tour at that period in their career, as well as organising all the practical details. The agent is also a link between the artist's manager and the concert promoter (see below). They are paid a percentage of the band's profits from the tour – anything from 5 to 30 per cent – or alternatively, a retainer, i.e. a monthly salary.

What does a booking agent do?

The agent negotiates with concert promoters (see below) to get gigs for their client. If the band/artist is just starting out and trying to get established it's the agent's job to persuade promoters to give their client a chance to perform. If the band is unsigned (as is often the case) they do this by emphasising past live triumphs, showing past press coverage and promising (often rashly) the attendance of music journalists who in reviewing the gig will, as a byproduct, also plug the venue and possibly the promoter.

In the case of bigger, more successful acts – who tend to arrange live dates or tours around the release of a new album – the boot's on the other foot and the agent will find their work is now in deciding which of several competing promoters it will be best to go with, and trying to maximise the fee, and the billing (i.e. top of the bill or third support – this gets particularly pressurised and ill-tempered in the case of festivals, which is why you may find it odd that your favourite band has been beaten to the headline slot by someone ostensibly less famous or marvellous).

Agents for bigger acts will also negotiate with the record company to reduce the costs to the promoter of staging the gig (security, staging, endless bottles of Cristal . . .). For example, they might agree to joint poster campaigns, joint radio adverts with the record company to promote the album at the same time as the gig, or even US-style 'street teams' – gangs of young hipsters lured by the promise of free concert tickets and t-shirts into handing out flyers and talking up forthcoming gigs.

It's more complicated than it sounds – for example:

Venue capacity: do you book a venue which you know your band will easily fill, perhaps leaving people unable to get in? This will create the 'buzz' of a sold-out gig and help with hyping the band up. Or do you optimistically book a slightly-too-large venue and hope they fill it, giving each potential fan the chance to see the band live and be persuaded? Each case has to be judged individually.

Ticket price: agents work with local promoters (see below) to set a ticket price. In the case of provincial pubs

361-373 City Road
London EC1V 1PQ

Phone: 020-7278-3331
Fax: 020-7837-4672

CONTRACT #:

Agreement made this date, ? by and between (hereinafter referred to as Artist) and Promoter A (hereinafter referred to as Promoter). It is understood and
agreed that the Promoter engages the Artiste to perform the following engagement upon all the terms and conditions hereinafter set forth:

ARTIST: **Band A**   100% HEADLINE.
VENUE: **Venue A** ,

   Phone: Fax:

DATE(S):   **4 Oct 2003**
        Set Length at Artist's Discretion.

TICKETS:

Quantity		Grs Price	Comp/Kills	Deduct	Net Price	Discrptn	No. Days/Shws:	1 / 1
1,800	@ £	15.00			12.77	Adv	Load In:	TBA
					0.00		Snd Chck:	TBA
					0.00		Doors Open:	TBA
					0.00		Showtime(s):	TBA
					0.00		Onstage:	TBA
GP:	£ 27,000.00		Capacities		Merchandising		Ages:	TBA
VAT:	17.5%		Per Show: 1,800		Artist sell:		Curfew:	TBA
Net:	£ 22,978.72		Total tkts: 1,800		Build sell:			

TERMS: **£ 9,500.00 Guarantee**
            VERSUS 85% nett whichever is greater (+ VAT)
            PLUS Artist agrees to provide and pay for S&L and monitors to meet with Artist's specifications and approval.

**ADDITIONAL
CLAUSES:**   Promoter shall provide and pay for, as per Artist's specifications and approval, at no extra cost to Artist, any and all rider requirements.

OTHER ACT[S]:   Support   60%SG   £ 100.00

PAYMENTS: £4,750 Deposit to this Agency by certified cheque or bank wire only due by: 04/09/2003

      The balance of the guarantee shall be paid to Artist or Artist's representative immediately prior to the performance via cash only.
      All overage monies are due to Artist immediately following the performance herein via cash only.

IN WITNESS WHEREOF, the parties have executed this Agreement on the date first above written.

                                     Promoter A

X _____   X _____
                                       272 St Vincent Street

                                                       Fax:
                                    CONTACT :

The Agency Group Ltd. is acting as Agent and not as Principal and as such accepts no liability for any
acts, failures, errors or omissions on the part of the Principal.

Directors: Neil Warnock (Managing) and Geoff Meall, Members of the Agents Association. Registered in England No. 2517741.
VAT Registration No. 645 4625 28

Figure 5a. Booking agent's contract for a live performance.

Contract Addendums

Contract #:

The Provisions of this Contract Addendum are deemed incorporated in and part of the Concert Performance ("Engagement") identified below.

Artist:	**BAND A**
Date of Show[s]:	**4/10/03**
Venue:	VENUE A.

1	The Artist(s) reserves the right to stipulate the supporting attraction at a fee of £100 to be paid by the Promoter.
2	The Artist shall receive 100% Top Billing and the Artists' logo shall be used in ALL advertising.
3	The Promoter shall guarantee first class security at all times to ensure the safety of the Artist(s), auxiliary personnel, instruments and all equipment, costumes and personal property, during and after the performance. Particular security must be provided in the areas of the stage, dressing rooms, all exits and entrances to the auditorium and the remote mixing console. Security protection is to commence upon the arrival of the Tour Manager and equipment on the premises.
4	It is agreed and understood that the Promoter will pay the Artist's caterers the sum of £1,250 in cash (local currency) on the day of the engagement.
5	The Promoter will ensure that no recording of any sort or description either audio or visual, and for any purposes shall be made of the Artist(s)' performance, and will likewise ensure that no broadcast for radio, electronic media, webcast or television is made of the appearance and no filming of any sort of the performance takes place without prior written consent from the Artist.

Figure 5b. Booking agent's contract for a live performance.

and clubs this is often just the set entry fee to the venue and won't be changeable. However, in the case of larger acts and venues a price has to be set that is both reasonable and within the market average, and also making the most profit for all concerned. You mustn't make your band look cheap, but nor must you rip off the fans. Often a deal between the agent and promoter isn't struck until the last minute – a particularly hot band who've just cracked the Top 10 might be worth a lot more on the night of the gig than they were two months earlier when the gig was first planned.

After all costs have been deducted (door staff, sound engineers and crew, resident technical staff, food and

361-373 City Road
London EC1V 1PQ

Phone: 020-7278-3331
Fax: 020-7837-4672

CONTRACT EXPENSES

Printed: 10/10/03 - 1:19pm

Artiste:	**Band A**	Contract # Issued
Showdate(s):	**4 Oct 2003**	
Venue:	**Venue A**	

Ticket Price (s):	£ 15.00	--	--	-- --
Venue Deduct(s):				

Tickt Surchrg(s):	Phone:	Remote:	Box Office:
Capacity:	2,400	Sellable Cap: 1,800	
Gross Potential:	27,000.00	Taxes: 17.50 %	Net Potential: 22,978.72
Promoter:	Promoter A		
Note:	Facility deductions are included in the ticket price on the face of the ticket. Ticket surcharges are not.

EXPENSES   *Mark to the right of variable denotes amounts used in agency estimates and deal calculations below.*

	Amount	Description		Amount	Description			
						Artist Guarantee	£	9,500.00
Ads Nat £	300.00		Phone/Fax	20.00		Support	£	100.00
Ads Local	2,000.00	Scottish	Piano				£	
Ads FlyPost			Police				£	
Ads Radio			PRS	668.25			£	
Ads Leaflets	400.00		Ptuner					
Ads Poster	750.00	Inc artwork/dist	Rigger			**VARIABLES**		
Backline			Runner	150.00	Inc petrol	*Rent Guarantee*		X
Barricades			SecPvt	1,300.00		*Rent Cap*		X
BoxOff	80.00		SecT-sht			*Rent %*		% X
Catering	1,250.00		Setup			*Rent [ph]*	£	X
ChairRent			S&L			*Tkt Cmsn %*		% X
Cleanup			Spotop			*Tkt [ph]*	£	X
Damage Dep			Spots			*Tkt Cmsn Cap*		X
DressRooms			Staff	150.00		*Insur %*		% X
Eletrician			Stage			*Insur (ph)*		X
Elecpower			Stghnds	1,000.00		*C.C.%*		0.00 % X
EquipRent			Stgmgr			*C. C. [ph]*	£	X
Firemen			Tkprnt			*C.C. Cap*		0.00 X
Forklft			Tksell				%	% X
Furntr			Tktake				£	X
Groundtrans			Towels	50.00		*Total Variables*		0.000
HseExp/Nut			Venue Hire	2,000.00				
Ins Liab	80.00		Ushers			*Total Fixed Exp:*	£	20,428.06
Ins Cancel	259.81		Utilities					
Loaders			Catering	70.00	Assistant	**ESTIMATES**		
Medic	200.00					Break Even	£	20,428.06
Misc	100.00					Break Even Units		1,600
Monitors						Break Even %		88.89
PayTx						**DEAL CALCULATIONS**		
Parking								
Permits						**Artist %**		**85 %**
Deal Notes:		**Subtotal Exp** £		10,828.06		*Walkout Potential*	£	10,243.06
						Walkout %		44.58 %

Figure 5c. Booking agent's contract for a live performance.

drink 'riders', marketing . . . the list can be endless) the money from ticket sales is split between the band/artist and the promoter on a ratio of around 70:30 in the artist's favour. The agent then gets between 5 and 30 per cent of the band/artist's fee. Sometimes bands play for a 'guaranteed fee', meaning a set price however successful or poorly attended the gig is.

Major booking agencies include Primary Talent, International Talent Booking, The Agency Group Ltd and Helter Skelter.

GETTING IN THE DOOR
See Chapter 2 for more general suggestions on getting a job.

Practical experience will be more valuable than anything. Do you ever organise gigs at your student union, or in your local pub or nightclub? If not, start. It doesn't have to be the event of the decade, or even a money-spinner. Just the practical experience of organising a band, maybe a manager, maybe a promoter, record company or even just the pub landlord or college authorities will build relationships with other players in this field and impress a potential employer. If you're at college, run for social secretary or entertainments manager, or to be on the Ball Committee – anything that'll get your hands dirty in the live music field and look good on your CV.

Booking agents must be salesmanlike, self-confident and persuasive – sometimes phoning them directly will win respect as they'll know you're no shrinking violet.

The **Agents Association** (see Useful Addresses) represents entertainment industry agents in the UK and offers a very useful online directory of contemporary music agents at www.agents-uk.com. The **National Entertainment Agents Council** is a similar organisation with a smaller database of music agents.

A first job with an agency will often be on a training basis as a trainee booker/agent or agent's assistant, learning the business by dealing with contracts, organising work permits, diary management and general admin, before building up to booking college gigs and smaller pubs and clubs. Trainees also act as scouts for new talent – if an agent spots an act they like they will contact the record company or manager to find out if the band has or needs an agent.

Alternatively, if you set up as a one-man (or woman) band and do well, an agency might one day poach you and your bands.

Case study: Andy Woolliscroft, Primary Talent

'A love of music and a sabbatical post at uni as social secretary helped me to start off in the music industry as a very, very poorly paid assistant to an established agent who had sold me bands when I was a social secretary. In fact, all my breaks appeared via agents I had dealt with at uni. So whereas what you know is important, who you know is essential.

'Each year I booked larger tours – initially for artists represented by my boss – and slowly, as I grew more confident, I took on my own clients. I booked their shows and applied the knowledge I had picked up via my bosses. The only world I had was in gigs and music. Now

I'm a director and shareholder in a big agency and represent big international clients and have respect and status within the agency/ promoter world.

'The best bits of the job include the pride, and the respect given to me by clients – people who you admire for their amazing talents and who you are probably a big fan of (sometimes when I'm in some grand hotel in an amazing part of the world sitting talking to a big star I have to pinch myself). Also the pleasure of being part of a successful tour, knowing that it was me who put that audience together with that artist in that place and everyone had an amazing time – and the pleasure of making your client very successful. The money's good at this level, too. Worst is the lack of loyalty in the business and the way clients are misrepresented by other parties such as managers and record companies who then blame the agent. Telling your client bad news and never getting thanked for doing a good job is also tough. The hours are not family-friendly either.

'My advice to young people wanting to get a job with a booking agency is: be prepared for a long, hard struggle for no money at the start, and if you are lucky, and good, the pay-offs can be wonderful. But the love of music has to be paramount.'

CONCERT PROMOTERS

What is a promoter?

Closely linked to the role of the booking agent as described above, a concert promoter books bands and venues and sells the tickets, does the advertising, promotion and press, deals with lighting, security and stage equipment (if it's not already in place, which it tends to be) and – most importantly – deals with the box office at the end of the night, sharing the cash out and paying the band. They often operate out of one venue – it's more efficient for them to focus their energies on one pet venue where customers are regular and their reputation is established. On average promoters take a cut of 30–40 per cent of profit after all costs.

A promoter deals with an agent; often if the agent has a good roster of artists a promoter will take anything and everything offered. Others are more discerning and carve their own niche regardless.

What does a promoter do?

A typical day in the life of a regional music promoter

10 am	*Arrive in office. Deal with dozens of new emails from bands, their agents or managers asking for gigs.*
11 am	*Open post and listen to the demos sent in by the above – most of them unsolicited.*
12 noon	*Write press release for an upcoming concert, researching band info and digging out glowing press quotes.*
1 pm	*Email bands playing next week about equipment (can they share a drum kit with the support act to save storage space backstage?), while supplying directions to the venue and contact details.*
2 pm	*Spend afternoon designing, printing, photocopying and cutting posters and flyers for upcoming concert, and dealing with last-minute details.*

---

5 pm	*Arrive at venue for tonight's gig, armed with posters and flyers for future events to stick around the walls and tables.*
6 pm	*Sit in on load-in (when the bands arrive and carry equipment in) and soundcheck (when the bands have a little practice to check they're going to sound OK – the headliners always go first).*
7 pm	*Hang out with bands and feed them.*
9 pm	*Watch gig, be on hand in case of hiccups.*
11 pm	*Curfew. Divide up box office takings and make sure everyone gets in the right tour bus home . . .*

National/major music promoters include the well-known Metropolis Music, as well as Harvey Goldsmith's AMP, and Vince Power's Mean Fiddler. An excellent grounding and a leg-up into the world of music promoting are guaranteed if you're lucky enough to get a job with one of them.

Regional/independent music promoters – it's not all big fancy London offices and stadium venues. There are dozens of smaller outfits across the British Isles running regular gigs at smaller venues. Most promoters specialise in a particular genre of music, or venue – London-based promoters Serious, for example, handle mainly cutting edge contemporary classical music in London's artier venues.

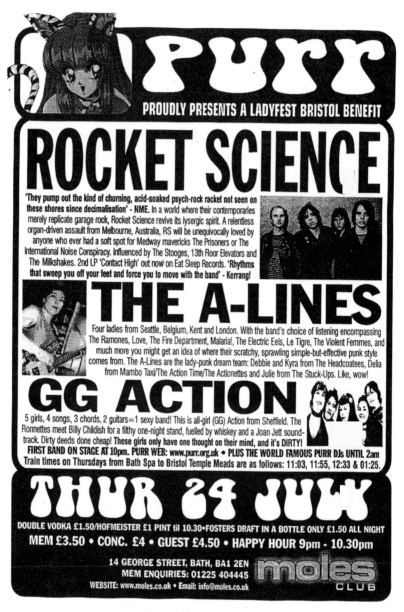

Figure 6. Concept poster.

Getting in the door

A keen eye and ear for what gig-goers want are essential. Do you go to many gigs yourself? Do you have a good idea of what sells and what doesn't? We all know Robbie Williams tickets will be like gold dust compared to your brother's thrash combo. So have a think instead about which local bands or DJs would sell out in your town and which would end up playing to three people and the bartender? If you don't know, forget it – you clearly don't have enough direct knowledge of the live music experience. Whether you're planning concert promotion as a solo career, a part-time hobby or hope to convince the suits at a major company that you have what it takes to be their hot young rookie you'll need to be brimming with ideas for live concerts that will raise the roof, and make money.

Do some of your own gig promotions. If you're at college have a go at being social or entertainments secretary, or join the Indie Society, or the Jazz Club or the orchestra ... anything like that. Try to get involved in different types of live gig: rock bands, soul singers, DJs. If you're not at college, is there a local pub or club that you could suggest booking bands for? You will need to be numerate – you'll be calculating costs, profits and percentages a lot of the time so if you don't know how to do percentages on a calculator, you'd better find out.

The **Concert Promoters Association** (CPA) is a trade organisation that can offer suggestions and information to those interested in promoting gigs within the UK.

Case study: Tim Orchard, Purr Productions

'I started off as a record buyer at the age of 5, and was in bands from the ages of 14 to 29. While I was in bands I wrote for punk fanzines in London and also for the regional press, alongside my day job. I got into promoting because no one else was doing it around my way (Bath). I'd have to go to London to see the bands I liked and so many nights I'd have to ring into work to say I was stuck at the station in London and wouldn't make it in the next morning.

'One day a friend was offered the job of promoter at Moles Club in Bath but he didn't want to do it, so he suggested me. The venue owner knew me from my days in a band, and as a local reviewer, and thought I'd be really good at it. I've been doing the job for three and a half years now. For the first gig I ever promoted I was given the email addresses of all the agents in the UK – I got zero response as it was over the millennium celebrations and no one was at work for days. So I went out and bought a single on an indie label, liked it, rang the number printed on the back, spoke to the record company, got the manager's number, agreed a fee and that was that.

'I still have a day job so I don't sleep much. All my leisure time is spent researching bands. We regularly get approached by record labels for our A & R knowledge. People offer us regular nights at other venues.

'My advice to someone just starting out would be, do what you believe in – if you believe in it someone else will too. Don't try to anticipate trends; don't just try to book bands you've read about in *NME*. Bring in local bands that are compatible with out-of-town headliners. Buy fanzines. But have some kind of method to your madness and be consistent in what you offer audiences, so they want to come down to your gigs and see what you've got on this week. Convince venues you know what you're talking about, that you know what's out there and how to convey it to an audience. Your job's to find out what's happening, not what's happened.'

TOUR MANAGERS

What is a tour manager?

When the booking agent and promoter have done their bit the tour manager enters the picture. Only established, better-known bands/artists have the luxury of one of these. A tour manager is a bit like a teacher on a school trip, only instead of a class of rowdy nine-year-olds they're dealing with musicians – who can be every bit as rowdy. They are hired by either an artist's manager (see Chapter 6) or a record company as soon as the decision is taken to go on tour.

What does a tour manager do?

A lot. A tour manager ushers and mothers artists from venue to venue, from town to town, or from country to country and makes sure everything that needs to be in place for a gig is in place – i.e. booking crews of roadies (see below); organising transport, work permits if necessary and hotels; and being on hand 24 hours a day during a tour. They are given a budget, out of which must come the wages of everyone hired for the tour plus hotels, flights, trucks for the gear, food and drink. They write up the itinerary and distribute it to everyone who'll need it. They'll sort out everyone's *per diems* (i.e. daily pocket money), obtain foreign currency, deal with homesickness and inter-band squabbling, liaise with promoters and report back to the artists' manager with accounts at the end of the tour. They also liaise with the record company and ensure their charges fulfil any promotional duties such as radio interviews in the town where they're playing. Oh, and – readers of a delicate nature should look away now – they fend off or usher in groupies. (Groupies aren't covered in this book. Read *I'm With The Band* by Pamela Des Barres instead.)

Getting in the door

You'll need to be a tough cookie with an authoritative approach and the ability to motivate. Many of the same skills associating with teaching or working with children, come to think of it.

You'll also need to be happy with the prospect of spending most of your time away from loved ones and calling a bunk in a malodorous tour bus 'home'. Most tour managers are ex-roadies (see below) or managers (see Chapter 6). If you have experience of this sort contact record companies and managers.

See also Chapter 2, Getting a Job.

ROADIES

What is a roadie?

Know what a 'C' wrench is? Like the look of those snazzy t-shirts with 'CREW' emblazoned across the back? Roadie is the affectionate name for road crew or backline technicians. They are basically techies providing services for touring bands/artists, ranging from truck drivers to piano tuners.

They may be hired for tours or one-off gigs by artists' managers (see Chapter 6) or tour managers (see above). Alternatively, in the town of the gig, local roadies may be hired to help out by the promoter (see above) as local crew.

(NB: Roadies are not to be confused with groupies.)

What do roadies do?

The rather outdated stereotypical view of a roadie is of a surly, monosyllabic, overweight, mullet-sporting hod-carrier straight out of the film *Spinal Tap*. In fact they are highly skilled technical experts without whom the show simply would not go on. Nowadays roadies tend to be specialists in one discipline or another.

They assist from the rehearsal stage onwards, up to and beyond the final gig of the tour. Some work on the sound, others the lighting, others the stage design, or instruments or rigging (the wires everything hangs from at large concerts), security or transportation (a.k.a. van drivers and bus drivers). On larger shows there can also be costume, make-up, catering and more. On full-blown live music extravaganzas (e.g. Robbie Williams at Kneb-worth) there will be video technicians, plus pyrotechnics and laser experts. Accordingly, the work can range from an evening's lugging amps around a small venue for a one-off gig, to years on the road, setting stages up for gigs as early as 8 am.

What you need to know

Most roadies are self-employed, which means there's not much job security and incomes fluctuate. Many lifelong roadies with decent incomes still find it hard to get mortgages and other forms of credit. However, in 2003 folk star Billy Bragg and the band Coldplay launched a trade union for roadies: the Roadcrew Provident Syndicate is a branch of the GMB, one of the country's biggest trade unions.

Getting in the door

Many roadies are keen musicians themselves, but chose not to follow the performance route, either because they realised they didn't have what it takes or never found the right band members to make up a hit band with. They do, however, have excellent musical knowledge and technical skills. Being a roadie allows them to perform and be a player, but in a different way. Others got into the field because they once helped out a friend in a band and it grew into a hobby that grew into a career.

The basic requirements are that, because of licensing laws, you will need to be at least 18 years old, and due to the long hours and tough, physical work you'll also need to be fit and strong. It helps enormously if you are a people person – no one wants to spend weeks or months or even years on the road with someone they can't stand. And anybody not punctual, sober and fully committed to the job won't last long. A clean driving licence is also a huge advantage.

It's much harder nowadays to get taken on as a roadie with no experience. So grab relevant experience wherever you can:

- At school or college, join the stage crew of the drama club. Working backstage, working a spotlight, keeping a mic from feeding back, sweeping floors, winding cables and getting shows ready are all ways of determining if a roadie's life is for you, and a great learning experience and place to make contacts.

♦ Failing that, volunteer to help with ALL kinds of live events round your way. Yes, that means your little brother's school play, the village panto, fashion shows, anything. Or try to get some work experience at a theatre or large concert hall or an events management company.

♦ Talk to roadies at gigs (pick your moment, i.e. not when the singer's mic has just snapped).

This will make you a much more reliable proposition when you then:

♦ Meet local bands at school, college, bars, clubs, festivals, etc. and offer to help them out for nothing – this is where most roadies get into the business. Who knows . . . maybe that nu-metal band you just helped carry all their gear out of their mum's Freelander will remember you when they sign to BMG and go stellar. Or perhaps they'll just tell someone else you're pretty handy, who'll tell someone else who'll give you a proper paid job one night.

♦ Ask your local venue if they need any help on the crew front. With a bit of luck you'll end up doing bits and pieces of lifting and carrying for them and they'll hire you as 'local crew' next time a band swings into town.

♦ Consider a college theatre course in stage lighting, sound production or stage management. Lists of these are available from the BPI and the Production Services Association (PSA). Find your area of interest (sound, lights, etc.) and concentrate on it.

◆ Read the *NME*'s 'musician wanted' ads. Sometimes bands will advertise for crew.

Top tip

Get in with the right people. Discounted membership of the Production Services Association (PSA) is available to students or people whose main income is not through working in the music industry. Amongst other things it offers the quarterly industry newsletter *BackStage*, subscription offers to other industry magazines, a monthly email newsletter plus privileged access to the PSA website (**www.psa.org.uk**) which very usefully offers industry news and developments, a chat forum and features a list of approved training courses in backstage, technical, staging, lighting and sound. It also advertises some vacancies and the list of members is a helpful contact list when sending on-spec letters. It's also worth having a look at the Professional Lighting & Sound Association (PLASA) website (**www.plasa.org**).

Music Journalism

In this chapter:

◆ What do music journalists do?

◆ Things you need to know

◆ Different areas of the music press

◆ Highs and lows

◆ Getting in the door

WHAT DO MUSIC JOURNALISTS DO?

Ah, music journalists. The luckiest people on earth. Or 'scum' to the legions of disgruntled artists out there who've been at the receiving end of their sharp tongues. The music press is the filter between you, the consumer, and the record company seeking to empty your wallet. The first impartial, critical view you're going to hear about a new record is from a music journalist. They are therefore pretty influential.

Music journalism comprises, amongst other things:

◆ **Features** on **bands/artists** involving an interview and photos

- **Features** on **musical trends** or current news

- **News items** – who's gone platinum, died, signed to a new label, been arrested for throwing peanuts at an air stewardess, etc.

- **Album/single reviews**

- **Gig reviews**

- **Q&As** – straightforward question and answer pieces

- **'Think pieces'**, in which a journalist expresses their opinion on a matter, personal experience or theory.

Music journalists can be full-time staff members but are usually freelancers – which is how you, as a newcomer, would start out.

At its best, music journalism will entertain and assist you in your musical purchases; at its worst it will infuriate and annoy and make you think 'I could do better!'. Well, maybe you could – if you think so, read on.

THINGS YOU NEED TO KNOW

Music hacks today refer fondly to the time immortalised in the film *Almost Famous* in which the journalists were as powerful as the bands they wrote about, when information, gossip and insight was passed freely from musician to writer without a stern, cautious PR person reining the artists in, as they do today, and when pretty groupies were as keen on the humble scribe as they were on the hunky bassist.

Lester Bangs was the most famous rock journalist of all time. In more recent years the likes of Nick Kent, Charles Shaar Murray and Julie Burchill have enjoyed a high status, while broadcasters like Miranda Sawyer have risen from the ranks of music journo to TV celebrity. Ageing pop stars Chrissie Hynde and Neil Tennant were also once music journalists.

Yet, as the landscape of the consumer press has changed, so has the job. No longer is music journalism the exclusive domain of the specialist magazine ('inkie' was a word once used for the music mags printed cheaply on newspaper that used to leave ink all over your hands). Nowadays virtually every publication you can think of covers music in some form or another. Specialist mags were decimated in the 1990s as title after title was axed or saw its circulation dip dramatically. And yet surprisingly, the early years of the new millennium saw a flurry of new titles such as *Bang*, *Word*, *Rip And Burn* and *X-Ray* spring up against the odds (and no doubt the exasperated handwringing of their accountants). Sadly, three of these newcomers quickly folded, prompting renewed pessimism over the health of the music press.

With the rise in importance of the artist manager and press officer, music journalists are no longer as free as their 1960s–1980s predecessors were to tell readers the unexpurgated truth about something. Interviews become political footballs; promotional albums are kept under lock and key for fear of piracy. Many feel the role of the music journalist is being whittled away as more and more people download advance copies of albums off the internet.

And yet there is still a noble purpose behind it all. Many music journalists assert that there is a need for them – otherwise consumers will believe everything the record company tells them, i.e. that an album is fantastic when it plainly isn't. There's also an evangelical element: if a journalist can introduce you to a piece of music that changes your life they'll die happy.

DIFFERENT AREAS OF THE MUSIC PRESS

Tabloids

Here music coverage tends to be lumped in with general showbiz gossip, featuring bands either high in the charts or soon to be. Reviews tend to be brief one-liners telling you little you couldn't have guessed for yourself already. The chances of writing for one of these are very slim unless you already happen to work in tabloids. Freelance possibilities: poor.

Broadsheets

At the posher end of the spectrum, these often take a more highbrow approach to music, with fewer jokes, less swearing, and using well-established writers on a weekly basis (sometimes daily in the case of big concert reviews). It is the hardest of the areas to break into, as writers tend to have long experience on a well-established publication and be a 'name' readers will recognise. The same tends to go for the bands they cover. Famous faces are common; undiscovered newcomers are rarely first lauded in a broadsheet. Freelance possibilities: poor.

Pop/teen/women's magazines

For example: *Smash Hits*, *Top Of The Pops Magazine*, *Just Seventeen*, *Marie Claire*. Lumped together because the coverage tends to be of very mainstream, commercial acts and household names. Freelance possibilities: reasonable.

Specialist music magazines

The weekly magazines *Kerrang!* and *NME*, and the monthly glossies *Q*, *Mojo*, *Uncut*, *Gramophone* (classical), *Echoes* (urban) and others come into this category. Each has a slightly different focus – some are more conservative or mainstream than others, some specialise in a single genre – but they all like to think they 'create' trends as well as follow them, 'discover' bands as well as react to them, and they carry large review sections and plentiful 'new' acts. These are where you'll find such purple prose as 'the strangely joyous sound of unbearable heartache morphing into light-headed relief'. Freelance possibilities: reasonable.

Regional press

A great way in. Is there a local listings magazine for your region? Bristol and Bath's *Venue* and Manchester's *City Life* are two of the best. Alternatively, does the local paper run a weekly music page? Check out their music and listings pages and offer your services to the music/arts editor. Chances are a time will come when nobody fancies a trip to the Dog and Turnip to see the local skiffle band who have been promised a review – and, hey, is that your telephone we hear ringing? Another point worth mentioning: they're almost always exceptionally nice people who, unlike their London counterparts, might actually answer their phone once in a while and speak to you like a fellow human. Freelance possibilities: good.

Internet sites

Obviously the BBC or MTV websites are out of the question if you're starting out, but do a spot of surfing and you'll be staggered at the amount of dotcoms floating around – some more respectable than others – offering music coverage. Check out www.drownedinsound.com, uk.launch.yahoo.com, www.soundgenerator.com and www.contactmusic.com for starters. Maybe you'll be writing for free for an editor who works from his bedroom and being read by about 12 people. It doesn't matter. If you're just starting out, small websites can be excellent experience and will prove to a future employer or commissioning editor that you are committed. Freelance possibilities: good.

Fanzines

These are the home-made-looking A5-sized rags sold at gigs and second-hand record shops. They tend to be anarchic, nutty and very leftfield. You'll be expected to write for free and to fit in with the tone, but the artistic licence tends to be whopping, and there are cred points to be had if the fanzine has a notorious reputation. A contact number or address of the person behind it ought to be tucked away on the pages somewhere, or ask the person who sold it to you. Alternatively, set up your own. Freelance possibilities: good.

THE HIGHS AND LOWS OF WORKING IN MUSIC JOURNALISM

Highs

◆ Free CDs, gig tickets, merchandise.

◆ Lots of parties, showcases and after-show parties where drink flows freely (go to too many of these, however, and it's called 'ligging' and the perpetrator a sad 'ligger').

◆ A lot of fun. This is one of *the* most wonderful jobs in the world.

◆ A certain degree of reflected glory and glamour.

Lows

The lows are worse for a freelancer than a staff member.

◆ There are many more music journalists than work available so competition is fierce and work can be threadbare.

◆ Awful money, as little as 8p a word in some cases.

◆ Hate-filled emails and letters from affronted readers, PR companies and even bands . . .

GETTING IN THE DOOR

Conventional wisdom has it that you can't get anywhere in journalism without a journalism degree. Nonsense. While this may be true in the world of hard news (interviewing politicians about inflation rates, say), the music press is bursting with people who'll tell you they made it there by having:

- a passion for music

- a nerd-like knowledge

- the ability to write

- gritty determination to get something, *anything*, published.

A journalism degree might help but won't be enough on its own: if you're up against another candidate's two well-written reviews in a small local listings magazine your journalism certificate won't be worth the paper it's written on. Also, if you're over-qualified, your would-be employer would have good cause to worry you'll end up leaving to pursue a career interviewing politicians about inflation rates . . .

The long way round would be to follow the traditional journalism route (journalism qualification, job on a local paper, and gradually work your way around to music) but if you are only interested in writing about music this would be daft. But you won't get a full-time job at a magazine or newspaper without having experience under your belt. So you need to **freelance first**, or at the very least write for free for a school/college newspaper (start your own if there isn't one), fanzine or website.

Practise writing. Describing music is like describing the indescribable. Try writing a 200-word review of your favourite album and see. If you can do it, and enjoy it, you'll do OK. If you find it too hard, give up now.

Read. Get hold of all the music journalism you can, from the pop section of the *Telegraph* to the college newspaper. What's good; what's bad? Why?

Select your targets. Be realistic – you're not going to get a commission from *The Times* unless Daddy's the editor. The *Sun* won't be interested in you unless you've got an exclusive interview on tape in which J-Lo confesses she's in love with Prince Charles. Start low and humble. Local press is a good start, or fanzines, or at a push a magazine whose album reviews run into the hundreds and gig reviews are spread across the country (this is one area in which being outside London can help).

Find out who is likely to **commission work from freelancers**: reviews editors on a specialist music magazine, for example, or a music editor on a lifestyle mag. Ring them maybe once, if you simply must, but leave it at that. Don't hassle them, as they get hassled all day long by PR companies as it is. The preferred method of communication tends to be post or email.

Write reviews of live gigs and albums in the style of one of the publications you'd like to write for and send them off with a polite introductory letter.

The best music journalism is honest, knowledgeable, well-informed and streetwise. Ideally it's also funny. Don't mention yourself in the review at all: no 'I', 'me' or 'my'. Readers don't want to hear about you, they want to know if they will like the music or not. Hang on, I hear you cry, all my favourite music journalists talk about

Live round-up

FAHRENHEIT 451 / THE ENGLISH PRICES
THE FLEECE, BRISTOL (THUR 2 MAR)

● The English Prices open brilliantly with a song all wriggly-riffed and light on its feet. A song, in short, that deserves rather more than to have platitudes such as "Come on, let's go!" hollered over it like Bono circa 1984. From there it's equally unwise to descend into a plodding rock we must dutifully term 'melodic'. Really smart, economical drummer, mind – find your own voice, chaps, because he'll obviously keep up with anything you can throw at him. The bassist and lead guitar/vocalist of F451 leap to and fro like tennis racket-wielding, pose-striking pre-teens in a bedroom. A good thing, of course, and the main man has two more things on his side: he can clearly play that thing to grade Shit Hot, doubtless knock you out a quick 'Flight Of The Bumble Bee' if the occasion demanded it, and spits out lines in a manner half-redolent of Jello Biafra. "Everything you know is wrong," he sings, which isn't strictly true – the aged hack knows an aspirant Green Day when he sees one. No ground broken, for sure, but conviction carries a charm all of its own. (Julian Owen)

Figure 7. Review of live appearance from *Venue* magazine.

themselves, and often to funny or entertaining effect. But these are established writers, on certain magazines and they are allowed to. Budding newcomers aren't.

If you honestly think you can write (and others back this up) and you really want to write, **keep trying**. Don't be put off because the first batch of reviews you send is ignored. Were they in the magazine's 'house style'? Did you send them to the right person? Probably they just don't need any more contributors at the moment. Try elsewhere. Then try your first choice again. Staff change all the time, and one reviews editor might be more accommodating to you than their predecessor.

Eventually you'll be given some work to do. That's when you can start to build up your work and all-important clippings file and call yourself a music writer.

Top tip
Unlikely as it might seem, judging by some of their own hilariously pretentious musings, employers in the music press loathe pretentiousness. Do not, on pain of death, namedrop, boast or brag about pop stars you may have met, been to school with, or once had a reply to a fan letter from. Your application will end up in the bin, and if it's in an interview, boy will your ears burn on the train home as they tumble about laughing over your pathetic urge to impress with the tale of how you once bummed a cigarette off the bass player from The Farts and now he's your best friend . . .

Case study: Chris Salmon, *Time Out* magazine

'I've loved music since I was really little and I'd say that's the most important thing if you're looking to work in the music industry. If you're getting into the industry for the glamour or the parties or the associated cool, then you're doing it for the wrong reasons and it'll probably show.

'So, for me, it was more a case of just loving music and gigs and then eventually falling into writing about it. I was talking to someone at a student party who turned out to be music editor for the college magazine and he said I should try writing some stuff for them. So I did reviews and interviews for them for about a year. Then, after I graduated I wrote about music for some regional listings magazines, as much for a hobby as anything else, while also working for a charity full-time.

'After I'd got a fair bit of experience with regional magazines, I wrote to a few bigger places to see if I could write some stuff for them. *Time Out* asked me to come in for a day to help compile the listings and write a couple of reviews and I must've done okay, because they asked me back and I built it up until I started full-time. I realise now that people are always on the look out for someone who is enthusiastic, knowledgeable, hard-working and humble enough to do the dreary things without complaining – so I must've fit that bill.

'I built up the number of days I was coming in as freelance cover – I still had my full-time office job at this point so I had to come in on my holiday time. Eventually I was getting so much work that I gave up the office job and came into the magazine full-time, first as a freelancer, then on a temporary contract and then eventually as full-time staff. After being listings assistant for a couple of years I applied for the job of deputy music editor and got it. Two years later I became music editor.

'My current job entails writing album reviews, live previews and interviews – anything from a short listing about a band's first gig in some toilet venue to a 1,800 word cover feature on Kylie, Oasis or Madonna. Aside from writing I have to plan feature ideas, commission pieces from other writers and liaise with press officers to find out what's coming up. I also do guest spots on TV and radio as a music expert, which is usually a good laugh.

'The best bit of the job is actually the same as the worst bit – you get hundreds of free records sent to you every week. In many ways it's a dream come true to get all the releases ages before they come out, but then you start to get so many that you actually don't have time to listen to them all! The other thing is that you're doing something you love as a job and it can sometimes be hard to just switch off and listen to a record without thinking what you'd write about it. These are small quibbles though, I've flown all over the world to interview most of my heroes, so I'm really not complaining!

'The most important advice I could give any aspiring music hack is just to get practice as a writer with a student mag, a regional magazine or a website. There's so many places out there that if you're keen, you should be able to get something. Also, be confident in your opinion and learn how to justify it. If you like something that everyone else hates (or vice versa) then you're going to need to be able to explain why!'

Recording Studios: Record Producers, Sound Engineers and Studio Managers

In this chapter:

◆ About recording studios

◆ Highs and lows of working in recording studios

◆ What record producers do

◆ What sound engineers do

◆ What studio managers do

The places pop stars always claim to be when they've been out of the charts for a while, recording studios are where recorded sounds (music and spoken word) are made, resulting in a master tape which is sent to the record company to be made into records.

Usually they consist of one or more 'mixing' rooms and one or more 'live' rooms. Larger studios might also house rehearsal space. Record companies or bands/artists pay by the day to use them; they cost upwards of several hundred pounds a day depending on the facilities offered.

Mixing room: this is where the producer and sound engineer (see below) work their magic, using a mixing desk, any digital sound generators, and controlling and recording the sounds being made in the . . .

Live room: a soundproofed room where the artists play their instruments. There's usually a separate booth for the vocalist (you've probably seen these in a few pop videos).

Artists' lounge: where artists and sometimes staff hang out when they're not actually required in the live or mixing rooms. This is usually where you'll find the loos, Playstations, sofas, magazines, pool tables, TV, coffee machine, thumb-twiddling girlfriends and boyfriends and so forth.

A far cry from the flashy steel-and-glass offices of major record companies, studios are usually far more discreet places, tucked away on ordinary streets (e.g. the famous Abbey Road studios), in basements, back rooms and back alleys – you could walk past many of them without registering what they were.

Some studios are known as 'residential'. These are hidden away in the countryside and offer accommodation for people using the facilities. Others belong to artists themselves and are situated within their home (or Peter Pan-themed fantasy world if your name is Michael Jackson).

THE HIGHS AND LOWS OF WORKING IN RECORDING STUDIOS

Highs

If working on the technical side you have an enormous amount of artistic influence and it can be as creatively satisfying as being a musician yourself. The money can be extremely good. Producers can earn tens of thousands of pounds for recording an album, and top engineers are also well rewarded.

Lows

Not recommended for claustrophobics or outdoor types, as the 16-hour days locked in a small, windowless, artificially-lit space can really drive you stir-crazy. It can also get stuffy and smoky and it's impossible to go outside to stretch your legs.

Many in this field are freelance and work on a project-by-project basis, so the work can therefore come through in fits and starts, which is nerve-wracking if you've got rent to pay. The pay is also very low when you're starting out as something like a studio assistant – £8,000 salaries are not uncommon.

RECORD PRODUCERS

What is a record producer?

The role of the record producer is absolutely integral and cannot be overstated when it comes to the creating of a band/artist's sound and the making of hit records. So it often seems rather unfair when a producer's handiwork is credited to the band or artists instead. It is producers who, in the majority of cases, turn a decent song into a great, commercial one – or turn sows' ears into silk purses in the case of some of the fluffier pop stars . . . As a mark of their importance they are, however, usually very well-renumerated by the record companies, who hire them on a project basis. They can become famous names themselves: e.g. Nellee Hooper, Trevor Horn, William Orbit.

As is the case with virtually every job mentioned in this book, the more successful/important you are, the more shots you can call. So, novice producers without much track record must tout their wares in the form of demos of past work to record company A & R departments and try to get some work, while a well-known super-producer can waltz directly up to artists they admire and ask to produce their next album. If the artists like the idea and have enough clout with their label this will generally go ahead (e.g. Trevor Horn with Belle And Sebastian's sixth album).

What do record producers do?

Record producers are hired (often through an agent or manager if they are particularly successful) by A & R departments of record companies (see Chapter 3) for projects (i.e. to record a single, or all or some of an album). Projects can last anything from one day to months and even years. Sometimes producers are also hired directly by unsigned artists and/or their managers for the purposes of making a demo.

In the case of an album, the first thing a producer will do is sit down and talk ideas through with the artists, listen to existing demos, pick out good bits and weak bits and decide what needs to be worked on. The producer will also select a sound engineer to work with (see below). There may then be a rehearsal period known as 'pre-production' in which songs to be recorded are thoroughly practised, fiddled about with, and any problems ironed out.

When the producer is ready to begin the recording sessions, each member of the band usually records their part separately.

During the recording the producer sits at the mixing desk (usually a 24-track desk, but it can be as many as 48 or as little as eight if they're after a basic, rough-and-ready feel) working alongside the engineer. But it's not all technical; just as important is steering the artists through the recording session, deciding what order to record songs in, suggesting changes in the playing/singing or even lyrics if they think it's necessary and keeping everyone focussed on and enthusiastic about the job at hand.

After recording, the music is 'mixed', i.e. the volume levels are balanced on each track and any extra sounds are added in. When everyone's happy (and this can take a while as artists will have their opinions too about how loud the guitars should be, or how long the intro should last) the final master is delivered to the record company for the A & R department's verdict.

Getting in the door
Record producers normally start out as assistant engineers, progressing to engineers (see below). There's little

chance of leaping straight into the producer's seat without climbing the ladder this way; you simply won't have the technical know-how, experience, maturity or diplomacy required.

However, some producers start out as musicians – producing is the favourite occupation of former pop stars when they get too old or unfashionable to get on *Top Of The Pops* themselves and don't fancy running a pub.

Courses in sound engineering or music technology contain a 'production' element but this alone won't make you a record producer. You'll still need to start as an engineer, or at the very least teach yourself the way around a mixing desk and get plenty of hands-on experience, like this rising star.

Case study: Dimitri Tikovoï, record producer

'I started making music when I was a child, out of passion and fun. At the time I could only see the outside aspect of it, which was a mysterious world, almost like a cartoon, where everything seemed to be quite distant from the reality. Music has always been either an entertainment form, a communication form (or in a few cases a research form), but the industrial aspect of it is quite recent and is not necessarily something that you see from the outside.

'Working in the music industry mixes two different feelings. One is the appeal of creating music that has the potential to be heard by a great number of people and therefore, as a producer, to try to push the limits of what is conventional. The other is the business and industrial side of it, which comes with the dark side of any business that needs to generate large sums of money without caring much for the product (in this case the artists) that it is exploiting. So as a producer, musician, or even if you work at a record label, you always find yourself torn apart between two realities.

'I started playing drums when I was seven, and was playing with bands by the age of 13 when I also bought my first computer and eight-track recorder. I then studied jazz and classical percussion and kept on playing live for other people. From what I earned from playing live and programming for other artists I bought more and more equipment to build my own studio. I didn't go to any engineering school, so everything I've learnt was from working with other people or experimenting by myself.

'When I was 17 I produced my first record for a major record company. I was a hard-working person and because of my unconventional background (most producers come from a sound engineer field) I started to get more specialised work. Luck has a very important place in all this, plus the fact that you shouldn't lose focus on what you believe and try to make everything possible to get your own sound and find a different way to approach things. Determination and love of what you do are the key factors.

'I started working quite young and had plenty of time to make many mistakes. You have to work hard, stick to what you are good at and believe in it and be patient. I am now working for bands and artists such as Placebo, John Cale, Michael J. Sheehy, Gary Numan, Goldfrapp, Marc Almond, Tram, Keith Flint and collaborative work with producers like Flood or Paul Kendall.

'The best thing about the job is that you learn every day from the people you work with, so it keeps you creative and you're always challenged. The worst thing comes with the requirements of the business, and the money factors.

'My advice to young people wanting to get into record production? Don't do it for the wrong reasons. It is a very long and difficult path which involves a lot of work, a lot of patience and a lot of struggle.

'Do it only because you feel passionate about music. The reality is that you'll probably have to work very hard for a very long time for very little reward at first, so the only thing that will keep you going is what you'll be learning in exchange and the privilege of meeting and working with interesting people. Do it for the fun and the rock 'n' roll. Forget about the sex and drugs, you won't have time and you won't be able to afford it anyway.'

SOUND/RECORDING ENGINEERS

What is a sound engineer?

Working closely with the producer, the sound engineer is often inseparable from, but not quite as 'senior' in the recording studio pecking order, as them. The engineer works on the technical side of a recording and tends to be the quiet one with the furrowed brow, sitting patiently fiddling with knobs while the producer is enthusiastically exhorting the bassist to take it 'once more from the top' through the studio intercom.

What do sound engineers do?

They look after all the studio equipment, setting it up at the start of the recording session and dismantling and checking it all again afterwards. They set up sound levels and dynamics (the loudness and softness of instruments) and acoustics within the live room. They then operate the mixing desk and/or recording software and any digital recording equipment during recording, and mix the different recorded tracks together onto the master tape. They then check the tapes, label them, assemble all the information on the recording needed by the record company and do anything else the producer needs them to do with regard to the recording.

Getting in the door

You will need:

◆ to be technically minded

◆ to have the requisite technical/electronic/electrical know-how

◆ in-depth musical knowledge or, even better, the ability to play an instrument yourself

◆ an ear for pitch, timing and rhythm

◆ diplomacy and tact

◆ courage to be creative when its required.

Bear in mind also that there's little room for egos in this field – the precious or moody need not apply.

There are over 200 courses covering sound engineering (often called Music Technology or something similar) at colleges and universities around the UK, ranging from MAs to BTECs, full-time and part-time, and everything in-between. Check those that are accredited with the **Association of Professional Recording Services** (APRS). When it comes to convincing a studio you have the wherewithal to come good for them, even a GCSE in electronics will be better than nothing.

Try to get work experience at a studio – find details in your local phone directory. London's famous Abbey Road and the beautiful Air Studios are just two of the most prestigious studios, and are used by all the main record labels and big stars. As such they are, predictably, regularly flooded with enquiries from wannabe studio hands. So if you're a total newcomer, forget them altogether and see if there's something smaller near you. At a smaller studio outside London which specialises in local bands' demos, radio commercials and jingles, the chances of getting a look-in and actually twiddling some knobs yourself are infinitely higher – you might even be allowed to do something other than refill the toilet roll holders and make coffee. A year of that and *then* you might be in a position to send Pete Waterman your CV.

Failing this, try work experience at a hospital radio station, offer to help out roadying for a local band or venue, or get work experience with the sound engineers of a big theatre (see also Chapter 7 on jobs in live music).

If you strike gold and a studio takes you on, an entry-level job will be as an assistant engineer or studio assistant ('tea boy' or 'tea girl' in the less enlightened studios!).

STUDIO MANAGERS

What is a studio manager?
Studio managers look after the studio, rather than the recording itself. It's an administrative/marketing role rather than a creative one.

What do studio managers do?
They have various duties. They try to get new business (and retain regular customers) for the studio using whatever marketing/advertising/phone means they can to

persuade A & R people at record companies to bring them business.

They negotiate fees with record companies, take bookings and keep the studio diary full to bursting and well-organised so that everyone knows who's recording what and when. They look after human resources: hiring staff, paying them, generally being the boss.

They ensure all equipment is properly maintained and fixed if necessary, and hire anything else that's needed. This is particularly important for the good reputation of the studio – if they don't have a swanky, up-to-date mixing desk, producers and engineers won't enjoy working with them and will therefore advise the record company that's footing the bill to choose somewhere else next time.

They look after the day-to-day running of the studio including making sure office supplies are available (from photocopy paper to boxes of DAT tapes), answering the phones, dealing with the post, etc.

They also need to be able to step in and help out if an extra pair of hands is required during the recording, be this helping the engineer find the wah-wah pedal, or bringing the singer more hot Ribena.

Getting in the door
You'll need to be a good multi-tasker as you'll often be doing three or four different things at once, with producers, engineers, assistant engineers, pop stars, receptionists and A & R coordinators all vying for your time and help.

You also need a keen business sense as you'll be the one out there pitching for work for your studio: there is fierce competition amongst studios for work from the major record companies.

Studio managers often start as receptionists and work their way up, but are also sometimes ex-musicians or producers who have built their own studio and want to run their own ship.

Work experience is a great way to begin – see also Chapter 2 for more information on getting a job.

OTHER JOBS YOU MIGHT FIND WITHIN A RECORDING STUDIO

◆ Receptionist

◆ Technical director – in charge of the equipment and technical side of things

◆ Catering staff

◆ Rehearsal room coordinator – some studios have rehearsal rooms which are booked out to record companies and bands/artists separately from the recording rooms.

Top tip
Second-hand eight-track recorders can be picked up very cheaply in the classifieds or in musical equipment shops. Get to grips with one of these and practise recording your friends and family on

their guitars or pianos, and work your way up to offering your services (for free to start with) to local bands needing demo tapes. Many ace albums are still recorded on eight-track so don't feel it's necessarily an inferior machine to a huge mixing desk. Become an eight-track wizard and the rest will follow more naturally . . .

10

Music Retail

In this chapter:

- ◆ What is music retail?

- ◆ What do music retailers do?

- ◆ What you need to know

- ◆ Different types of music retail outlet

- ◆ Different types of job

- ◆ Highs and lows

- ◆ Getting in the door

WHAT IS MUSIC RETAIL?

Music retail is the sale of records, in shops, to the general public. Not only has working in this field proved a most fertile breeding ground for some of the top record company execs and music journos of today, but it can also offer an exciting and important career in its own right if you take it further than the Christmas job.

Once upon a sepia-tinted time all music retailers were independent, innocent and not especially commercially-minded music-lovers with a steady business. Then, in the

1970s, along came Our Price, a new breed of music retailer that stocked in bulk and sold at low prices. Their aggressive market stance changed everything. Nowadays CDs and other music products are sold in more places than they ever have been. As well as the independent specialist record stores that always have the coolest carrier bags, the scowliest staff and were immortalised in the film *High Fidelity*, we now buy CDs from the internet, supermarkets and garages.

As well as CDs, many shops also sell videos, DVDs, computer games, calendars, t-shirts, music magazines, concert tickets, and even audio equipment like personal stereos and DJ gear.

Retailers pay record companies/distributors a '**dealer price**' for CDs. This can vary but is always somewhere between what the record company has paid to make the CD and what a customer will pay for it, i.e. the retail price. Dealer prices are the subject of almost all communication between retailers and their suppliers. For the retailer, the difference between the dealer and retail prices is their all-important profit margin.

WHAT DO MUSIC RETAILERS DO?

Stock control

Orders for stock are placed by the shop staff either by phone to a distributor's telesales staff (see Chapter 3), to a visiting sales rep, or through the EROS in-store ordering computer system which is linked up to the distributor. Some stores also order from wholesalers – organisations that service smaller outlets with smaller quantities of stock from many different labels and distributors ('Only one copy of the new Limp Bizkit please, this is Hay-on-Wye after all'). The ability to spot the gaps in your repertoire, and conversely, when to delete from stock, is important. This can be a tricky aspect of the job. How to satisfy demand for a new title without grossly over-ordering? Getting the balance right in terms of diversity of stock and striking the right buy-in versus turnover ratio (i.e. how many you order versus how many you'll sell) is an art.

Stock processing

This is basically filling the racks. It can be fun when you're handling brand new titles, but tedious when it's the 200th *Carpenters Best Of* you've handled that year. New releases are delivered the Friday before the release date and retailers are under strict instructions not to display or sell them before then. The retailers then stick the price labels on and 'process' or rack them.

Store displays

This means assembling any new 'point of sale' material: dumpbins, posters, etc. In the case of the chainstores, this point of sale material – as well as matters such as shelf space and display (or 'racking') of CDs – has been organised in advance with the record company, which strikes mutually beneficial deals over it. Yes, it is all a little shady . . .

Faulty product and returns

Most retailers send back to the distributor/record company a certain amount of 'returns', i.e. CDs that haven't sold. This will include faulty goods that have been returned to the shop by the customer.

Other duties
These include selling to the customer at the counter, balancing up at the end of the day and keeping the counter tidy and useable.

DIFFERENT TYPES OF MUSIC RETAIL OUTLET

◆ **Specialist chains**: HMV, Virgin, MVC, Fopp

◆ **Multiples**: chain stores for whom music is just one of several types of goods, e.g. Borders, WHSmith, Woolworths

◆ Independent stores

◆ Supermarkets and garages

THINGS YOU NEED TO KNOW

Practices like piracy, illegal downloading and CD burning have hit retailers harder than anyone else in the music industry. Unlike record companies, they don't have many other avenues (like downloads, licensing, synch, ringtones, computer games, etc.) to fall back on to make extra money. As the daily unit turnover (i.e. the amount of records sold per day) drops, it becomes like trying to sell bread when there's a bloke in a balaclava giving it away free on the corner of the street.

Year after year, music specialists also lose more and more custom to supermarkets, multiples and chains (see above). (Next time you think of buying the new Sean

Paul at Sainsbury's – don't! Get it from the little shop round the corner with all the posters in the window.)

Many independent stores therefore survive by:

♦ specialising in the kind of product customers can't get at supermarkets or copy from friends. They will ditch the chart albums and specialise in dance music for example, filling the racks with rare releases and imports from small labels that fans go bananas for, but larger chains won't look twice at unless a customer actually comes in and pleads for it.

♦ offering better customer choice and service. They can't compete with their larger rivals on price – they aren't in a position to negotiate discounts from record companies because they don't buy enough, so they try to offer superior service instead.

'With the emergence of the "no-margin", chart-product-only supermarket approach, the independents are falling back on older artists who have had earlier material remastered and enhanced with extra tracks and visual media,' explains veteran music retailer Paul Lloyd (see Case Study). 'This is enabling them to persuade the enthusiast to part with his money again for an even richer experience than his initial one, and to broaden the minds of the younger enthusiast.'

However, lest we start thinking the non-indie stores have it too easy, it's worth noting that they are feeling the pinch too. Recent years have seen US giants Tower Records pull out of the UK due to lack of business, the respected Andy's chain go into administration and Australian chain Sanity (which bought Our Price – remember them?) closed its 110 stores here after just two years.

DIFFERENT TYPES OF JOBS IN MUSIC RETAIL

Sales assistant

This includes stock control and stock processing, serving customers, answering enquiries and working on store displays. In an independent store your enthusiasm for music will be more appreciated than in a chain as you'll often be the single point of contact for the customer, and you're likely to have regulars who'll want to discuss everything from old Cure b-sides to Sting's appearance on *Parkinson*. Also your knowledge of music and a good memory will be valuable with regard to stock enquiries – you won't have the computer systems of a chain where most enquiries can be dealt with by tapping on a keyboard. You'll also be expected to help out wherever needed in the shop, rather than stick to the one designated task you'd probably be assigned by a chain.

Buyer

This is the member of staff in charge of ordering up and stocking the shop with music of a certain genre – with bigger stores there'll be a dance buyer, a rock buyer, a jazz buyer, a world buyer, a folk buyer, a classical buyer … The amount ordered depends on how many copies they think the shop will sell.

Head buyer

Chains and supermarkets will normally have one of these for every genre of music, working usually from a central office, seeing record company reps and buying various amounts of stock for distribution to stores around the country.

Shop manager

This involves acting as a buyer, seeing reps, organising promotional events such a signings and live gigs and generally ensuring the smooth day-to-day running of the premises.

Owner

Same as the manager but can be more hands-off, and concentrate on expanding the business. Most managers/ owners spend less than one day per week on the shop floor dealing directly with customers.

HIGHS AND LOWS

Highs

You're literally surrounded by music all day. You get to hear all the new releases as soon as they are out. There's no better place to launch into a career elsewhere in the music industry, as you'll gain a knowledge of music and its consumers as broad as the Nile and end up knowing more about the current music scene than many A & R managers. Music retail attracts a wide and vibrant mix of individuals and is often a lot of fun to work in.

Lows

Job security can be shaky. Working weekends is often unavoidable. Plus, as with all shop work, you'll be on your feet most of the day and the job can be tedious.

GETTING IN THE DOOR

You'll need:

◆ an in-depth knowledge of at least one genre of music, and an awareness of musical trends

◆ to be a good team player

◆ a sense of humour

◆ good customer skills like patience and tolerance

◆ the ability to be methodical and good with systems.

High-street stores regularly advertise staff vacancies in their windows or on a vacancy board. Demand for staff increases enormously during busy trading periods like Christmas.

In addition to regular jobs, many of the chains and multiples also offer structured training schemes for various levels. HMV, for example, offer:

◆ Basic two-week work experience slots for secondary school pupils in their record stores.

◆ Foundation Modern Apprenticeship for school leavers which can result in a full-time job at the end.

◆ Graduate scheme: a year's training based in two separate stores learning initially in the first store about the various operations of the store and what all the staff do, and then learning about management in the second store. An assistant manager role usually follows thereafter. A degree and a certain amount of flexibility is required. Fifty places are available per year, and start dates are in April and September.

Apply online at **www.hmvcareers.co.uk**.

Those interested in graduate jobs at Virgin should send their CV and a letter outlining their areas of interest to head office (see Useful Addresses). Details of in-store vacancies can be obtained from the shop manager.

Alternatively, make friends with the staff in your local independent store (naturally, being a music fan you'll be in there every Saturday having a snoop around at the new releases anyway, right?). Let them know you're looking for work, and you know your stuff (that should be obvious already, right?). Take an interest in what they do. Ask how their day's going. Ask what's flying off the shelves at the moment.

A lot of people start in music retail with a view to moving into distribution, manufacture, and even A & R. If you want it to be, the world of music retail can be a stepping stone to another part of the entertainment industry or media.

You may, however, dream of managing or even owning your own store – in this case your shop-floor experience as an employee will need to be supplemented by grit, determination and steely self-discipline as well as astute business acumen.

The **British Association of Record Dealers** (BARD) is a well-respected and vociferously campaigning trade organisation for retailers and wholesalers of music, video, DVD and multimedia products (see Useful Addresses). Its website, **www.bardltd.org**, offers a very handy online database of record stores plus facts, figures and stats about record retailing that, as well as giving you a good overview of the business, will also impress employers.

Case study: Paul Lloyd, Warrior CD, Crystal Palace, SE London

'I always wanted to work in music in some way. I had a dabble at playing drums in a band, then did a bit of singing. I had aspirations to work in a studio, but the sheer volume of different bits on a basic mixing desk terrified me. I've always done a bit of DJ-ing and still play local bars, parties, etc. I have always read extensively about music, spent all my money on records and digested in its entirety every edition of the *Guinness Book of Hit Singles* . . . I went into retail in the late 70s after becoming a single man – very liberating. Felt I could pursue my personal passion without the burden of responsibility.

'A friend of mine, Andy Ross (founder of Food label) told me that Our Price were looking for staff at the branch he managed in Lewisham. I applied and went for an interview.

'At that time they were looking for young, confident, enthusiastic, trendy people. I obviously fit the bill (!) though Andy had to impress upon me the importance of not looking too smart, in case I scared them off. I started as seven-inch singles buyer.

'Realising that knowledge and enthusiasm would not get me promotion (hard-nosed commercial sense was more of a prerequisite) I moved on to an independent in the City of London. Initially I took an assistant position, but after a couple of years I was promoted to manager of the 'Popular' department. It was a very busy unit and my knowledge took a quantum leap forward due to the diversity of stock required.

'I felt restricted in some ways by working in an established outlet and, noting that the second hand/collectors market was beginning to boom, I then pursued my own enterprise, setting up a direct mail business of my own, and taking a stand at record fairs around the country. I happily scraped a living for two years. Then some friends offered me a job managing a new, independent retail outlet in Surrey. This was the beginning of a successful and fulfilling 10-year association.

'However, the business struggled. The outlet's position on a side street in a town with little else to draw the passing consumer meant that it really required a thriving direct mail side to increase the turnover, and/or specialist advertising in publications such as *Record Collector* to lure the enthusiast who was willing to travel further afield to find what they were looking for. I then applied for a management position in a local CD shop, specialising in chart and R & B CDs at low, high street prices. Part of my remit has been to inject the business with additional revenues, attracting a new customer base through the introduction of new sections, including a growing second-hand/indie section. In the current unstable music retail environment I believe the breadth of my knowledge has helped my current employer. We have been able to take advantage of as many local consumer trends and demands as possible.

'We take frequent trips to the US where we buy large amounts of new and used product covering a multitude of musical styles. However, as a small, independent retailer we are currently struggling to make sufficient sales in today's climate. The impact of the current rash of illegal copying and downloading, combined with price competition from local supermarkets and Woolworths, is applying enormous pressure on us. I am again considering, against all reason, going back to running my own small mail order business, possibly combining it with a small retail outlet, specialising in second-hand and collectable vinyl and CDs – for this is ultimately where my passion lies.'

Glossary

A & R a person or department within a record company that finds and looks after the artists.

advance the money paid to bands when they first sign a record or publishing deal. This has to be recouped (see below).

after-show private party after a gig, for industry folk and journalists, usually with a guest appearance from the band/artist.

back catalogue a record company's 'old stuff' as opposed to their new releases.

blag to get something for free just because you're in the business or have the requisite know-how.

budget the amount of money set aside for a project based on how much profit it is thought will be made, e.g. a marketing budget or tour budget. Must be strictly adhered to.

copyright the legal right to print, publish, perform, film or record literary, artistic or musical material.

dealer price the price at which record shops buy records from a record company.

'Dido demographic' coined by a broadsheet journalist, picked up by *Music Week* and now commonly used to describe the sort of customers who only buy one or two albums a year of safe, mainstream music but are nonetheless capable of creating multi-platinum-selling albums and global stars. Like Dido.

exploiting not as evil as it sounds (or is it?), this is the act of developing artists and selling as much of their work as possible.

genre a certain style of music, e.g. country, R & B, speed garage.

guest list a list of people allowed into a gig for free because they are important. Full of the words 'plus one' (see below).

indie/independent not part of a major corporation. Applies to record labels, publishers and stores.

ligger a derogatory term given to one who ligs (see below).

ligging going to too many industry parties, showcases and gigs to drink free beer.

load-in when a band arrives at a concert venue and carries all their equipment in.

majors the four big multinational record companies: EMI, Sony BMG, Universal and Warners.

margin the difference between money spent and money made.

merchandiser a company that makes t-shirts, badges, bags, posters, etc. featuring a band/artist's name/logo/picture.

networking making contacts, striking up useful acquaintances.

parts the raw materials for making a CD that are sent to the manufacturer, generally the artwork and the master tapes.

per diem a daily subsistence allowance doled out to each member of a touring crew, plus the band.

plus one a free ticket for two to a concert (as in 'I'm on the guest list: Zoe Ball plus one').

point-of-sale material marketing material given to shops to promote releases; includes posters, display stands, dumpbins, etc.

racking the strategic placing of CDs on a shop's shelves to ensure maximum visibility.

recoup to earn back your advance (if you're a band) by selling as many records as you are supposed to.

returns unsold records returned from the retailer to the distributor. Record companies dread these.

rider the food and drink provided backstage for a band or artists before a gig.

roster the list of artists signed to a record company, publisher, PR company or manager.

sampling pinching, with permission or otherwise, a snatch of music by another artist to put in your own song.

schmoozing buttering up, flattering (usually over lunch or dinner) and persuading someone to do what you want.

selling in what sales reps do when they talk shops into buying new releases.

shipping the delivery (not necessarily by ship) of stock from the manufacturer to the distributor.

showcase a private gig for industry and press.

soundcheck when bands tune up and have a little practice before a gig to make sure the sound is all right.

svengali a senior figure with enormous influence and status, traditionally aiding and abetting young innocents.

unit industry-speak for a CD.

Useful Addresses

Abbey Road Studios
3 Abbey Road
London NW8 9AY
Tel: 020 7266 7000
www.abbeyroad.com

Absolute Promotions & PR
Ground Floor (Rear)
34 Maple Street
London W1T 6HD
Tel: 020 7323 2238

The Agency Group
370 City Road
London EC1V 2QA
Tel: 020 7278 3331
www.theagencygroup.com

Agents Association (GB)
54 Keyes House
Dolphin Square
London SW1V 3NA
Tel: 020 7834 0515
www.agents-uk.com

AIM (Association of Independent Music)
Lamb House
Church Street
Chiswick
London W4 2PD
Tel: 020 8994 5599
www.musicindie.org

Air Studios (Lyndhurst)
Lyndhurst Hall
Lyndhurst Road
London NW3 5NG
Tel: 020 7794 0660
www.airstudios.com

Anglo Plugging
Fulham Palace
Bishops Avenue
London SW6 6EA
Tel: 020 7384 7373
www.angloplugging.co.uk

British Association of Record Dealers (BARD)
1st Floor
Colonnade House
2 Westover Road
Bournemouth
Dorset BH1 2BY
Tel: 01202 292063
www.bardltd.org

BMG Music Publishing UK
Bedford House
69–79 Fulham High Street

London SW6 3JW
Tel: 020 7384 7500
www.bmgmusicsearch.com

Boosey and Hawkes Music Publishers
295 Regent Street
London W1B 2JH
Tel: 020 7291 7222
www.boosey.com

BPI (British Phonographic Industry)
Riverside Building
County Hall
Westminster Bridge Road
London SE1 7JA
Tel: 020 7803 1300
www.bpi.co.uk

Career Moves
1st Floor
1–2 Berners Street
London W1T 3LA
Tel: 020 7908 7900
www.cmoves.co.uk

Carlin Music Corporation
Iron Bridge House
3 Bridge Approach
London NW1 8BD
Tel: 020 7734 3251

Chrysalis Music
The Chrysalis Building
13 Bramley Road

London W10 6SP
Tel: 020 7221 2213
www.chrysalis.com

Coalition Group
Devonshire House
12 Barley Mow Passage
London W4 4PH
Tel: 020 8987 0123

Concert Promoters Association (CPA)
360 Oxford Street
London W1C 1JN
Tel: 020 7491 9365

EMI Group plc (International dept)
4 Tenterden Street
Hanover Square
London W1A 2AY
Tel: 020 7355 4848
www.emigroup.com

EMI Music Publishing
127 Charing Cross Road
London WC2H 0QY
Tel: 020 7434 2131
www.emimusicpub.co.uk

EMI Recorded Music UK & Ireland
EMI House
43 Brook Green
London W6 7EF
Tel: 020 7605 5000
www.emirecords.co.uk/www.virginrecords.co.uk

The Entertainment Network (TEN)
Rabans Lane
Aylesbury
Bucks HP19 8TS
Tel: 01296 426151
www.ten-net.com

Hall Or Nothing
11 Poplar Mews
Uxbridge Road
London W12 7JS
Tel: 020 8740 6288
www.hallornothing.com

Handle Recruitment
4 Gees Court
London W1U 1JD
Tel: 020 7569 9999
www.handle.co.uk

Helter Skelter
The Plaza
535 Kings Road
London SW10 0SZ
Tel: 020 7376 8501

HMV UK
142 Wardour Street
London W1F 8LN
Tel: 020 7432 2000
www.hmv.co.uk

Independiente Ltd
The Drill Hall
3 Heathfield Terrace
London W4 4JE
Tel: 020 8747 8111
www.independiente.co.uk

International Music Publications (IMP)
Griffin House
161 Hammersmith Road
London W6 8BS
Tel: 020 8222 9222
www.wbpdealers.com

International Talent Booking
Ariel House
74a Charlotte Street
London W1T 4QH
Tel: 020 7379 1313
www.itb.co.uk

In The City
8 Brewery Yard
Deva Centre
Trinity Way
Salford M3 7BB
Tel: 0161 839 3930
www.inthecity.co.uk

LD Publicity
58–59 Great Marlborough Street
London W1F 7JY
Tel: 020 7439 7222
www.ldpublicity.com

Learn Direct
PO Box 900
Manchester
M60 3LE
Tel: 0800 101 901
www.learndirect.co.uk

MBC PR
Wellington Building
28–32 Wellington Road
London NW8 9SP
Tel: 020 7483 9205

MCPS (Mechanical Copyright Protection Society)
Copyright House
29–33 Berners Street
London W1T 3AB
Tel: 020 7580 5544
www.mcps.co.uk

Mean Fiddler Concerts
16 High Street
Harlesden
London NW10 4LX
Tel: 020 8961 5490
www.meanfiddler.com

Metropolis Music
69 Caversham Road
London NW5 2DR
Tel: 020 7424 6800
www.gigsandtours.com

Midem (UK)
Walmar House
296 Regent Street
London W1B 3AB
Tel: 020 7528 0086

Ministry Of Sound Recordings
103 Gaunt Street
London SE1 6DP
Tel: 020 7378 6528
www.ministryofsound.com

Music Managers Forum
1 York Street
London W1U 6PA
Tel: 08708 507800
www.ukmmf.net

The Music Market Ltd
2nd Floor
4 Paddington Street
London W1U 5QE
Tel: 020 7486 9102
www.themusicmarket.co.uk

Music Publishers Association Limited
3rd Floor
Strandgate
18/20 York Buildings
London WC2N 6JU
Tel: 020 7839 7779
www.mpaonline.org.uk

Music Sales
8/9 Frith Street
London W1V 5TZ
Tel: 020 7434 0066
www.musicsales.com

Music Week
CMP Information
United Business Media
8th Floor
Ludgate House
245 Blackfriars Road
London SE1 9UR
Tel (subscriptions): 01858 438893
www.musicweek.com

MVC
Congress House
Lyon Road
Harrow
Middlesex HA1 2EN
www.mvc.co.uk

National Entertainment Agents Council (NEAC)
PO Box 112
Seaford
East Sussex BN25 2DQ
Tel: 0870 755 7612
www.neac.org.uk

Pinnacle
Osprey House
New Mill Road
Orpington

Kent BR5 3QG
Tel: 01689 870622
www.pinnacle-entertainment.co.uk

Primary Talent International
2–12 Pentonville Road
London N1 9PL
Tel: 020 7833 8998
www.primary.uk.com/primary

The Professional Lighting & Sound Association
  (PLASA)
38 St Leonards Road
Eastbourne
East Sussex BN21 3UT
Tel: 01323 410335
www.plasa.org

PRS (Performing Right Society)
Copyright House
29–33 Berners Street
London W1T 3AB
Tel: 020 7580 5544
www.prs.co.uk

Production Services Association (PSA)
Centre Court
1301 Stratford Road
Hall Green
Birmingham B28 9HH
Tel: 0121 6937127
www.psa.org.uk

Rough Trade Records
66 Golborne Road
London W10 5PS
Tel: 020 8960 9888
www.roughtraderecords.com

Sony/ATV Music Publishing
10 Great Marlborough Street
London W1F 7LP
Tel: 020 7911 8200
www.sonyatv.com

Sony BMG
Bedford House
69–79 Fulham High Street
London SW6 3JW
Tel: 020 7384 7500
www.sonybmgmusic.co.uk

Total Home Entertainment (THE)
Head Office
Rosevale Business Park
Newcastle-under-Lyme
Staffordshire ST5 7QT
Tel: 01782 566 566
www.the.co.uk

Universal Music UK
PO Box 1420
1 Sussex Place
London W6 9XS
Tel: 020 8910 5000
www.umusic.com

Universal Music International
8 St James Square
London SW1Y 4JU
Tel: 020 7747 4000
www.umusic.com

Universal Music Publishing
Elsinore House
77 Fulham Palace Road
London W6 8JA
Tel: 020 8752 2600
www.universalmusicpublishing.com

Virgin Entertainment Group
The School House
50 Brook Green
London W6 7RR
Tel: 020 8752 9000
www.virgin.com

Vital Distribution
338a Ladbroke Grove
London W10 5AH
Tel: 020 8324 2400
www.vitaluk.com

Warner-Chappell Music
The Warner Building
28a Kensington Church Street
London W8 4EP
Tel: 020 7938 0000
www.warnerchappell.com

Warner Music UK
The Warner Building
28a Kensington Church Street
London W8 4EP
Tel: 020 7368 2500
www.warnermusic.co.uk

Warner Music International
83 Baker Street
London W1M 2LA
Tel: 020 7535 9000
www.wmg.com

Windswept Music
Hope House
40 St Peter's Road
London W6 9BD
Tel: 020 8237 8400
www.windsweptpacific.com

XL Recordings
1 Codrington Mews
London W11 2EH
Tel: 020 8870 7511
www.xl-recordings.com

Further Reading

Alan McGee and the Story of Creation Records Paolo Hewitt with Alan McGee (Mainstream Publishing, 2000)

Crosstown Traffic: Jimi Hendrix and Post-War Pop Charles Shaar Murray (Faber & Faber, 2001)

England's Dreaming: Anarchy, Sex Pistols, Punk Rock and Beyond Jon Savage (St Martin's Press, 2002)

The Faber Book Of Pop ed. Hanif Kuresihi and Jon Savage (Faber & Faber, 1996)

The Hip Hop Years – A History of Rap Alex Ogg with David Upshal (Channel 4 Books/Macmillan, 1999)

I'm with the Band: Confessions of a Groupie Pamela des Barres (Helter Skelter, 2003)

Let It Blurt – The Life And Times Of Lester Bangs Jim DeRogatis (Bloomsbury, 2000)

Lives of the Great Songs ed. Tim de Lisle (Pavilion, 1994)

Music Week Directory (CMP Information, published annually)

Mystery Train: Images of America in Rock and Roll Music Greil Marcus (Faber & Faber, 2000)

The Rough Guide to Classical Music ed. Joe Staines (Rough Guides, 2001)

The Rough Guide to House Music Sean Bidder (Rough Guides, 1999)

The Rough Guide to Rock ed. Mark Ellingham (Rough Guides, 2003)

She-Bop II: the definitive history of women in rock, pop and soul. Lucy O'Brien (Continuum, 2002)

This Is Uncool: The 500 Greatest Singles Since Punk & Disco Garry Mulholland (Cassell Illustrated, 2002)

Index